A Desired Past

A Desired

℃ THE UNIVERSITY OF CHICAGO PRESS

Past

A SHORT HISTORY

OF SAME-SEX LOVE

IN AMERICA

Leila J. Rupp

CHICAGO AND LONDON ❱

Leila J. Rupp is professor of history and a member of the
graduate faculty in the Department of Women's Studies at
Ohio State University. She is the author or coauthor of several
books, including *Worlds of Women: The Making of an International
Women's Movement* and *Survival in the Doldrums: The American
Women's Rights Movement, 1945 to the 1960s* (with Verta Taylor).

The University of Chicago Press, Chicago 60637
The University of Chicago Press, Ltd., London
© 1999 by The University of Chicago
All rights reserved. Published 1999
08 07 06 05 04 03 02 01 00 99   1 2 3 4 5
ISBN: 0-226-73155-3 (cloth)

Library of Congress Cataloging-in-Publication Data

Rupp, Leila J., 1950–
    A desired past : a short history of same-sex love in America /
Leila J. Rupp.
        p.   cm.
    Includes bibliographical references.
    ISBN 0-226-73155-3 (cloth : alk. paper).
    1. Gays—United States—History.   2. Homosexuality—United States
—History.   I. Title.
HQ76.3.U5R86   1999
306.76'6'0973—dc21   98-56542
                                                                    CIP

♾ The paper used in this publication meets the minimum requirements of
the American National Standard for Information Sciences—Permanence
of Paper for Printed Library Materials, ANSI Z39.48-1992.

For Verta

Contents

Preface

Every day, as part of my morning routine, I wind the German china clock that my grandfather gave my grandmother in 1902 to celebrate the birth of their first (and as it turned out, only) daughter, Leila. When Leila died in 1991, my father (her brother) inherited the clock. It chimed as my father cared for my mother in her last days, and when my father died two years later, my brother and sister simply assumed the clock would be mine. Each morning while winding the clock, I have thought about this book, since it begins with Aunt Leila.

The truth is that I don't know whether I would have had the courage to put all this in print had I known that Aunt Leila, my mother, and my father would read it. Yet I did tell my parents about the project, and I did write some of it literally at my father's bedside as he lay dying. When he fell asleep, I would pull out my books and laptop and try to distract myself. He would have understood, for he too experienced writing as joy and solace, and somehow he passed this gift along to me. As always, I need to acknowledge the enormous debt I owe my family for surrounding me with love, support, intellectual stimulation, and a passion for the past.

Without really knowing it, Marty Duberman inspired me to begin this project. Several years ago he asked me to contribute to the "young adult" series launched by Chelsea House. I was deeply immersed in my work on the international women's movement and didn't really want to put it aside, yet I was also enormously attracted to the challenge of synthesizing the history of same-sex sexuality for a general audience. The series went down the drain, though, when right-wing agitation caused libraries to cancel orders for any books published by Chelsea House. But in the end I got to have my cake and eat it too. I finished one book and started the other, and voilà, *A Desired Past* took shape.

I am greatly indebted to those from my present and past—some here only in spirit—for many of the personal stories I share in this book. I especially thank Leila, Diantha, Sidney, Walter, Margaret, John, Verta, Pippa, Carla, Cody, Lily, Steve, Donna, John, Phyllis, Kelly, Alice, Sushi, Milla, Scabola, Inga, Margo, Kylie, R. V., and of course Emma.

Needless to say, I couldn't have written this book without the brilliant and courageous work of so many historians who have excavated past lives and crafted the tales that make this synthesis possible. The notes and reference list track their contributions, but I feel the need to say an even bigger thank-you to all of them, and to mention especially Jonathan Katz, whose documentary histories have proved priceless; John D'Emilio and Estelle Freedman, whose *Intimate Matters* lighted the way; and several others whose research plays an especially important role here: Robert Baum, Brett Beemyn, Allan Bérubé,

Rudi Bleys, Nan Boyd, Kathleen Brown, Vern and Bonnie Bullough, George Chauncey, Blanche Cook, Madeline Davis, Allen Drexel, Marty Duberman, Lisa Duggan, Lillian Faderman, Trisha Franzen, Eric Garber, Richard Godbeer, Karen Hansen, Helen Horowitz, John Howard, David Johnson, Liz Kennedy, Elizabeth Knowlton, the late Marty Levine, Leisa Meyer, Joan Nestle, Esther Newton, Mary Beth Norton, Annelise Orleck, Michael Quinn, Tim Retzloff, David Reynolds, Anthony Rotundo, Charles Shively, Carroll Smith-Rosenberg, Marc Stein, Roey Thorpe, Richard Trexler, Sharon Ullman, Walter Williams, and Judy Wu. I am also grateful to those scholars—Alex Cofield, Susan Freeman, Lyn Hegarty, David Johnson, Liz Kennedy, Barbara Moum, John Weiss, and Judy Wu—who sent or lent me unpublished material and generously allowed me to quote from it.

John D'Emilio, Nancy Guzowski, Pippa Holloway, Joan Huber, Betsy Kaminski, Joanne Meyerowitz, Carla Pestana, Birgitte Søland, Marc Stein, and Verta Taylor read the entire manuscript and contributed all sorts of assistance, much of it way beyond the call of duty: moral support, encouragement, enthusiasm, expert advice, suggestions for specific revisions, and astute and thorough criticism. Heather Miller provided valuable research assistance and held my hand through the trauma of switching to a new computer program. I thank the many individuals at libraries and archives who supplied photographs and gave me permission to reprint them here. In particular, Karolina Garrett of the Northern California Gay and Lesbian Historical Society and Morgan Gwenwald of the Lesbian Herstory Archives went out of their way to help. When I could not find all the photographs I needed, Jack, Mark, and Tim stepped in. Alice Bennett's expert and inspired copyediting improved my prose immeasurably. And finally, Doug Mitchell encouraged me, took a chance on a project outside what the University of Chicago Press usually publishes, and entertained me with lively e-mail messages and his famous taste for good restaurants.

John Lennon and Paul McCartney's "In My Life," with its wistful remembering of places and lovers and friends, captures what I feel about the personal past I have put into this book. And it also furnishes the best line for Verta: There's no one compares with you.

One

INTRODUCTION: THINKING ABOUT

AUNT LEILA

*W*hen I try to explain to my friends why my aunt Leila was so important to me, I usually say that I'm her namesake, that she taught history, and that she lived with a woman, Diantha, for as long as I can remember. They were just like a married couple in our family. We visited them on summer vacations "down the shore," as we said in New Jersey, though they always rented their own apartment. They had one bedroom, with twin beds. They liked to drive to a spot overlooking the ocean and sit in their car reading. Sometimes they took me, and I sat in the back and read too. I wrote poems, and Diantha, who taught English in the same Pittsburgh high school where Leila taught, encouraged me. They always dressed similarly, but with certain regular differences: linen dresses with jackets, for example, but different cuts and colors (Diantha's red or yellow, Leila's blue or green). Diantha cooked and Leila washed the dishes, and they teased each other, both claiming to do most of the work.

They had other women friends who lived as couples, and when Aunt Leila first met my partner Verta, after Diantha had died, she took her aside, told her how glad she was that I'd found a friend, and asked whether Verta knew she too had had a friend. She called up her new friend, Mary, who came to meet us, and the two of them stood there arm in arm. But later Aunt Leila confided that no one suited her like Diantha.

The last time I talked with Aunt Leila she was eighty-nine, in a nursing home, having become extremely confused from what I'm pretty sure was a series of small strokes. I hoped she would talk about Diantha. My father, her younger brother, said she never mentioned Diantha, and he reported that shortly after Diantha died, several different people told him Diantha hadn't been very nice to Leila. When he repeated this to Leila she got furious and forbade him ever to bring up Diantha's name. I think this happened because the two women treated each other the way couples do, sometimes bickering or showing irritation, yet not everyone acknowledged them as a couple.

When I talked about Diantha, Leila didn't answer. In some ways she hadn't changed. She was still immaculately attired, in a dress and pumps, her hair done and rouge on her cheeks. She had the same derisive chuckle that used to mean she thought you were a little crazy, but now it may have simply covered her confusion. At one point she looked down at her hands, gnarled with veins, and said—as if she'd forgotten that her body had gotten old—that she'd just noticed how awful they were. When I complimented her on her elegant dress, she plucked the fabric in the front, looked down, and said, "This old thing?" And later she looked me right in the eye and said:

Aunt Leila (right), Diantha (middle), my mother, Sidney (left), and me (front), Stone Harbor, New Jersey, 1953.

"There's something I've been meaning to tell you. But I can't remember. Maybe I'll remember later."

Seven weeks later she died. I like to think she meant to tell me about Diantha. But maybe that's just wishful thinking.

I tell the story of Aunt Leila because I still don't know if she was a lesbian. For me she evokes all the complexities captured in the term "same-sex love and sexuality." She was a "lady," and a conservative one at that. To the outside world she was a "maiden aunt." I always assumed she would be horrified by the label "lesbian." My uncertainty about whether I can name as a "lesbian" a woman who chose another woman as her life partner but who as far as I know never embraced the identity underscores the historical debates about the nature of same-sex sexuality. What does it mean to say a woman was a lesbian? That she identified herself that way? That she "had sex" with another woman? That she was "in love with" a woman? That she saw herself in a conceptual category with other women who loved women?

It is, first of all, a question of evidence. I don't know anything about Aunt Leila's desire, sexual behavior, or self-conception. But of course we don't know about such things for most people in the past. And that's the problem. The difficulty of locating sources that document same-sex love and sexuality is legendary. Reflecting the modern Western association of women with love and men with sex, the evidence in the case of women, as the story of Aunt Leila so aptly illustrates, tends to reveal emotional attachments to other women. It's not that women never had sex and men never loved each other, just that our evidence is skewed. With regard to men, we have a lot more evidence of sexual acts, but we often do not know whether that behavior says anything about love or desire. Far too much of what we know about men's sexuality comes from criminal investigations or prosecutions, which ensure a particular construction of events. A man caught "in the act" with another man was not likely to proclaim his love for his partner, although one creative individual, the Dutch Calvinist minister Andreas Klink, convicted of sodomy in 1759, claimed that his attraction to men was natural because he had absorbed in utero his mother's longing for his absent father.[1] Had Klink's defense not failed—he was eternally banished, but at least not executed—perhaps we might have been left with other confessions of same-sex desire. Perhaps he might have started a trend in sodomy cases.

What is rare is the voice of a person speaking directly about her or his same-sex love, desire, or sexual acts. Such documents for the past require, first of all, literacy, which differed by gender, race, class, region, and period, and second, courage, to leave a written record of what societies variously viewed as crime, sin, or illness. Even if people kept diaries or penned love letters, too often they made sure to destroy them later, fearful of leaving a trace of their generally forbidden desires. So biographer Blanche Wiesen Cook reports that Lorena Hickok—who in one of her surviving missives wrote to Eleanor Roosevelt remembering "the feeling of that soft spot just north-east of the corner of your mouth against my lips"—after the first lady's death fed to the fire letters they had exchanged.[2] And historian Estelle Freedman records the terse diary entry, "The burning of letters continues," which alerted her to pioneer prison superintendent Miriam Van Waters's erasure of her correspondence with her beloved friend Geraldine Thompson.[3]

Even when people left their words on paper, others both protective and hostile have set out to censor the past. Scholar Martin Duberman tells of his long struggle to unearth the sexually explicit 1826 letters of James H. Hammond and Thomas Jefferson Withers, important conservative figures in the pre–Civil War South, in the face of massive opposition from the South Caroliniana Library.[4] In other cases, too, archivists, researchers, family members, and friends have sought to avoid "besmirching" the reputations of individuals who might be categorized as "homosexual."

So we do not always know as much as we would like about the lives and loves of people in the past, though historians have found evidence in all kinds of places. This is a work of synthesis, based on the painstaking research of dozens of scholars who have uncovered astonishing bits of evidence and crafted provocative interpretations of our history. Court cases, newspapers, letters, diaries, cowboy limericks, medical writings, reports of social reformers, blues lyrics, and for the more recent past interviews provide a wealth of fascinating detail or in some cases just offer frustrating glimpses of worlds of same-sex love and sexuality.

But suppose I had asked Aunt Leila about herself, and suppose she had said no, of course she wasn't one of those women, she just loved Diantha and had made a life with her. Then what? What it means that someone loved—or had sex with—someone of the same sex is not at all clear, even in the twentieth century. In previous centuries the meaning of emotional commitments or sexual acts can be even less transparent. In contemporary American society we often distinguish between "homosexuals" and "heterosexuals," with a category of "bisexuals" sometimes added in. If we today do not always agree about why people love and desire as they do—some look to biological factors and others to social explanations—our culture nevertheless has definite categories for sexuality. We also have a clear idea of what counts as a "sexual act." But it has not always been so, and it is not so everywhere. The problem for historians is that those ways of viewing the sexual world are not universal across time and place. That is, not all cultures have two or three categories for types of sexuality based on sexual-object choice—the preferred sex of one's partner in sexual acts—nor do they all even define the same acts as "sexual."

We shall see how much ideas about sexuality have changed, and how conflicting ideas have coexisted, even within the relatively short span of time since the beginnings of American history. But looking even farther afield may help illuminate the issues at play here. In the highlands of New Guinea, Sambia boys can grow into adulthood only if they swallow the semen of older men, so male initiation rites involve fellatio. Participating in such an act in either role is expected, is not deviant, and means nothing about one's "sexuality." And is the act itself even "sexual"? Is it significant that young boys become men by putting mouth to penis rather than by eating semen with a bowl and spoon?[5]

How we think about such questions—and there are no easy, agreed-on answers—shapes the way we interpret history. Certainly it is clear that in different times and places people have participated in acts that contemporary American society usually defines as sexual and deviant without their cultures' considering them either of those things. The concept of a "homosexual" person, defined by desire and sexual behavior, is a relatively recent historical development. (The "heterosexual," too, is of recent origin, as historian Jonathan Katz has so whimsically argued. Moreover, the first use of the word in the United States, in 1892, referred to "abnormal manifestations of the sexual appetite.")[6]

All of this explains why I avoid using the terms "gay" and "lesbian" or even "homosexual" to describe individuals who desired or loved or engaged in sexual activities with others of the same sex unless they lived at a time when those categories had been named and claimed. Instead I use "same-sex love and sexuality" to describe a wide variety of desires and emotions and behaviors throughout American history. Yet this does not entirely avoid the tricky conceptual problems, for the term "same-sex sexuality" still assumes that we know what is "sexual" and that, however diverse, acts and relationships between people of the same sex share some fundamental similarity. But does the "same-sex sexuality" of, for example, Martin Duberman's Jim Hammond and Jeff Withers belong in the same conceptual category with the "same-sex love" of Aunt Leila?

Within the world of historical scholarship there are some who would say yes, there is some core of commonality that transcends cultures and history.[7] Despite vastly different societal practices, they would say, some people have always desired and loved others of the same sex, and some always will do so. If we just look hard enough—for example, at those men in New Guinea who find the male initiation rites particularly pleasurable—we can find evidence that "gay people" have always existed.

Other historians—and I count myself among them— are more dubious about such comparisons across time and place.[8] At the opposite end of the spectrum from those who emphasize similarity, some scholars argue that we can understand an act of same-sex sexuality only in its own very particular context. Take the case of ancient Athenian society, long held up to either praise or scorn for its idealization of sexual relations between older and younger men. Rather than a haven for male same-sex desire, a number of scholars have argued, Athenian society was a place in which sexual relations expressed solely power, the power of older men over younger men, free men over enslaved men, men over women. To paraphrase Tina Turner, "What's desire got to do with it?"[9] As in the male initiation rites in New Guinea, an Athenian male's use of his penis was not necessarily about "sexuality" as we understand that term.

These are complex and confusing questions that run counter to our intuitive understandings of sexuality. The important point here is that sexuality is not a fixed essence, understood and practiced the same way across history and around the globe. Perhaps the best way to illustrate this is through a perceptive comment made by Pippa Holloway, a graduate student at Ohio State. In a class on the history of same-sex sexuality, we were discussing Anne Lister, an independent, mannish early nineteenth-century English gentlewoman, who kept an elaborately coded diary in which she recorded her numerous sexual affairs with women, some of them married.[10] We were talking about whether we might consider Lister a lesbian, and Pippa, who has little patience with transhistorical comparisons, pointed out that, just because the words are familiar, we can't assume we know what people meant when they called Lister "queer" or when she described herself as different because of her preference for women, any more than we can know what she meant when she said she felt "vapourish." I think Pippa is right, and yet . . .

I hope in this book to explain how a whole variety of people—boys accused of sodomy in the seventeenth century, cross-dressing Native Americans, nineteenth-century middle-class women who fell in love with each other with the full approval of their culture, and "fairies" on the street corners of the Bowery—were different both from each other and from late twentieth-century gay and lesbian Americans. But at the same time, by telling their stories within these covers, I admit to a conception that sees a potential for certain common patterns in same-sex sexual desires and acts, romantic liaisons, and gender transgressions across time and place. That is, I emphasize the "same-sex," when perhaps the people involved might have put the emphasis elsewhere. I include individuals who crossed the gender line even though some may not have desired or engaged in sex with others in physiologically alike bodies or, if they did, may not have considered their desires or acts as "same-sex." I do this because gender ambiguity or gender crossing raises the possibility of same-sex sexual desire and behavior.

To illustrate how people see the relevant categories differently, I'll conclude with my friend Carla Pestana's son, Cody. When Cody was about five, he and a girl from his school were playing with the family dog, Lily. The friend said, "I love Lily so much I wish I could marry her, but I can't, because she's a girl." Cody, wise beyond his years, retorted: "That's not the reason you can't marry Lily. You can't marry Lily because she's a dog." It's all a question of different takes on the relevant categories.

All of which is to explain why thinking about Aunt Leila is so difficult. She remains an enigma in a society that *has* named lesbianism. If we do not know what to make of her, or others like her, how are we to understand people who lived in wholly different worlds? Yet we need to comprehend the variety of desires and loves and sexual acts that make up our past because the very ways we think about gender and sexuality are a product of this history. Using the meticulous research of historians who have followed bread-crumb trails out of the forest of ignorance about sexuality in the past, I try to make sense here of the lives of diverse individuals who have rarely made it into our history books. Part of me is afraid Aunt Leila would have hated this book. But I keep hoping she wouldn't.

Two

IN THE BEGINNING: SAME-SEX SEXUALITY IN EARLY AMERICA

While I was in the midst of writing this chapter, I read a book that profoundly unsettled me. I had finished the section on Native American societies when I found Richard Trexler's *Sex and Conquest: Gendered Violence, Political Order, and the European Conquest of the Americas*.[1] The author, a scholar of the Italian Renaissance, had switched his sights to the Americas, and in his deeply researched and provocative study he turned upside down everything I thought I knew about "berdaches," biological males who dressed and lived as women among many of the indigenous societies of the New World. In Trexler's vision the cross-gender berdache is not the honored spiritual figure, living in a society with a more flexible understanding of gender, that most other recent scholars have described. Rather, the berdache stands as an emblem of the systematic child abuse and violent domination of the feminine that continues to plague modern society. Indeed, Trexler argues that military power and the very process of state building rest on both the literal and the metaphorical rape of men by other men.

I had no idea what to make of Trexler's book. I particularly could not imagine how I would incorporate it into this narrative. What kept popping into my mind was another book with an agenda, although an altogether different one. Just a few weeks before, I had picked up transgender activist Leslie Feinberg's *Transgender Warriors: Making History from Joan of Arc to RuPaul,* a personal and impassioned account of people in the past, including the berdache, who defied cultural boundaries of sex and gender.[2] In writing about "Two-Spirit" people—a rough translation of the variety of Native American words for cross-gender individuals—Feinberg emphasizes the spirituality, tolerance, and gender fluidity of native cultures.

There is simply no way to reconcile these two books. Although Feinberg's sweeping assumption that "transgendered people" can be identified across time and space violates my sense of the need to understand vastly different historical contexts, ultimately I found myself less and less convinced by Trexler's overall argument. He too emphasizes sameness across long stretches of time—in that sense the two authors do share something. It's not that I don't find Trexler persuasive when he says that, at least among some South American cultures, men who dressed as women were despised even before the arrival of the Spanish. I don't doubt his evidence, but I do wonder if it tells the whole story. In his account of same-sex sexuality there's no place for anything but rape and violence and domination. I'm sure that was there. But was it all?

I share my confusion because it illustrates the dilemmas of historical interpretation. History, for most historians in the late twentieth century, is not the one "true story." Rather, it is a story as best we can tell it, given the evidence, our own assumptions and values, and the perspective we take from our own place in a particular society at a specific point in time. If this is the case even for a relatively straightforward account of, say, a past presidential election—and I believe it is—then how much more is it true for a loaded subject such as sexuality? With this in mind, let us turn to a history of the momentous encounter among the cultures of America, Europe, and Africa.

The peoples who lived in the land that would come to be called America had diverse understandings of gender (that is, the social roles associated with being male or female) and of appropriate sexual behavior. They were often puzzled by the worldview of the first Europeans to traverse the Atlantic. These intruders had definite ideas about the differences between men and women and about what constituted appropriate sexual behavior for each, and these expectations often clashed with those of the societies they encountered when they set foot ashore. Likewise, Africans who had the misfortune to come into contact with Europeans through the slave trade confronted different concepts of gender and sexuality. In other words, competing sexual and gender systems (that is, ways of thinking about and organizing sexuality and gender) came face-to-face through the European invasion and the forced emigration of Africans. The ultimately dominant European system, with its rigorous condemnation of same-sex sexuality, was not the only vision of the world to have an impact on individuals living in what became the United States. Nor was that system unaffected by contact with Native American and African cultures.

I begin by considering Native American, European, and African sexual systems in order to show the different ways the societies the early "Americans" came from conceived of gender and same-sex sexuality. I then turn to colonial legal codes and evidence of same-sex sexual behavior among women and men of the settler colonies. As we shall see, engaging in same-sex sexual acts did not automatically identify a participant as a certain kind of person. Rather, religious and civil authorities focused on the acts, which they condemned as sinful and unnatural—perhaps more dangerous than other nonmarital and nonprocreative sexual behavior, but not qualitatively different. Most important, these were acts that any sinner might be tempted to commit. So even the victorious European system differed from modern Western notions of "homosexuality."

A "New World" of Sexuality and Gender

Although it is impossible to generalize about the diverse Native American cultures of North America, accounts of sexual expressiveness are common enough to paint a picture of a world that valued sexual desire and experimentation. Among the Powhatans, men might take multiple wives if they could afford to, and both women and men might end marriages with relative ease. In a rare hint of what Native Americans thought about their cultural clash with white settlers over sexuality, a male European observer in early Virginia reported of the Powhatans that "nothing appears to them more repugnant to nature and reason than the contrary system which prevails among Christians. The Great Spirit, say they, hath created us all to be happy; and we should offend him were we to live in a perpetual state of constraint and uneasiness."[3]

In the sixteenth century the Pueblo peoples of what would become New Mexico also practiced serial monogamy and valued sexuality as a vital and life-giving natural force. In Hopi rituals celebrating female sexuality and reproductive abilities, women danced naked in a circle, fondling clay phalluses, taunting the men with lewd songs and exposing their vaginas; they ended the ceremony by having sex with the men.[4]

Far east of the Pueblos and north of the Powhatans, the seventeenth-century Hurons, who formed a clan-based society in which descent followed the female line, considered premarital sexual relationships from puberty onward a normal expression of sexual desire. Girls as well as boys could initiate sexual relations, and if a girl became pregnant she could choose one of her lovers to marry. After a sort of trial marriage, a ceremony would cement the bond, which then became sexually exclusive but easily sundered. Such practices provoked the Jesuits working among the Hurons to condemn sexual freedom, especially among the young.[5] In this they echoed the Spanish in New Mexico and the English in Virginia, as is clear from a white man's description of a Powhatan ritual he little understood. "Thirty young women came naked out of the woods, only covered behind and before with a few green leaves, their bodies all painted . . . . These fiends, with most hellish shouts and cries, rushing from among the trees, cast themselves in a ring about the fire, singing and dancing with most excellent ill variety, oft falling into their infernal passions."[6] The nudity, the shouting, the "infernal passions" differentiated these lascivious and promiscuous "fiends" from the familiar "ladies" back home. The invaders had indeed landed in a "new world."

Whether sexual openness extended to same-sex encounters is more difficult to determine. The French Jesuit Joseph-François Lafitau, who lived among the native peoples of Canada, reported the existence of "special friendships" among young men that he compared to the sexual bonds between younger and older men in classical Greece. "These bonds of friendship, among the Savages of North America, admit no suspicion of apparent vice, albeit there is, or may be, much real vice."[7] Although we know no more about the nature of such friendships, or about sexual relationships between women, cultures that view sexuality in a positive light and permit childhood experimentation tend to be more likely to see adult same-sex sexuality as an acceptable emotional and erotic possibility, as long as individuals meet their reproductive responsibilities to the group.[8]

But it was not only nudity and sexual experimentation and same-sex friendship that separated Native American and European sexual systems. Rather, it was that a variety of cultures scattered throughout what would become the United States saw not two genders, but rather men, women, and a third category, what the Navajos called *nadle,* the Lakotas *winkte* (for biological males) or *koskalaka* (for biological females), and the Omahas *mexoga,* the terms referring either to transformation, becoming a woman or man, or to a "third gender," half man/half woman.[9] These were men who took on the dress and social roles of women and engaged in sexual relationships with masculine men, or women who dressed as and did the work of men and married feminine women. Their societies had a social and usually acceptable, sometimes even honored, role for them. Transgender individuals generally fulfilled both spiritual and social purposes in their societies, despite the evident skepticism of the contemporary observer Father Charlevoix, who noted in 1721 that "it was pretended that this custom came from I know not what principle of religion."[10] (Richard Trexler also doubts the claim that religion served as the source of cross-gender behavior.) Yet the Jesuit Jacques Marquette reported after his trip down the Mississippi in the 1670s that such cross-gender individuals "are summoned to the Councils, and nothing can be decided without their advice . . . . they pass for . . . spirits,—or persons of Consequence."[11]

The cross-gender role institutionalized same-sex sexual relations, even if sexuality was not the reason individuals crossed the gender line. Most men who took on the feminine role had sex with men of masculine gender, and cross-gender females often married and had sex with feminine women. Such sexual activities did not imply anything about the sexuality of the non-cross-gender partner. The sexual behavior in such relationships was conceptualized neither as same-sex nor as different-sex, but as something distinct from both. The Mohave language includes a term that refers specifically to the lovemaking of a cross-gender female and her partner, and the Lakotas have a word for male-male intercourse that is derived from the word for a cross-gender biological male. Until contact with Europeans, it seems that many Native American cultures with institutionalized cross-gender roles saw nothing deviant about sexual relations in this context. European censure changed some of that.

These "persons of Consequence" struck the Europeans variously as "men in womens apparell," "hermaphrodites," symbols of "effeminacy and lewdness," or "a devilish thing." Spanish explorer Álvar Núñez Cabeza de Vaca, a captive among the Native Americans of Florida from 1528 to 1533, observed: "I saw one man married to another, and these are impotent, effeminate men and they go about dressed as women, and do women's tasks."[12] Getting right to what they found the most horrifying, the European settlers called a man in women's clothes a "berdache," a French version of Persian and Arabic words meaning a young male slave kept for sexual purposes. Father Charlevoix denounced the Iroquois for "an excess of effeminacy and lewdness. There are," he reported, "men unashamed to wear women's clothing and to practice all the occupations of women, from which follows corruption that I cannot express . . . . These effeminates never marry and abandon themselves to the most infamous passions."[13]

Hernando de Alarcón, observing the Pueblo Indians in 1540, noted that berdaches "could not have carnal relations with women at all, but they themselves could be used by all marriageable youths."[14]

So when Spanish soldiers and explorers, French fur traders and Jesuits, and English religious dissidents and settlers crossed the Atlantic and stepped ashore, they truly entered a different world of gender and sexuality. Although many of the European invaders did their best to exterminate offending Native American gender orders and sexual systems, along with Native American peoples themselves, they did not entirely succeed. And they were undoubtedly affected by what they encountered.

Libertines, Seafarers, Mollies, and "Roaring Girls"

If the Europeans could not conceive of a person neither clearly male nor clearly female, and if they vigorously repressed same-sex sexual experimentation and relationships, that did not mean that gender transgression and same-sex sexuality were unknown in the worlds the explorers and settlers came from. Despite long-standing civil and religious condemnation and the threat of execution, individuals did engage in same-sex sexual behavior in a number of contexts, sometimes without the punishment that the law prescribed or without even the disapproval of their neighbors.

Following an old tradition in European culture, elite men of the nobility or clergy might engage with relative impunity in sexual acts with younger or lower-status men in an atmosphere of privileged sexual license. What was critical here—as in many other contexts—was the sexual role a man took in a particular encounter. To play what is misnamed the "active" role, meaning to make use of one's penis in oral, intercrural ("between the thighs"), or anal sex, did not necessarily label a man as deviant. To penetrate another was considered "manly," which is why the receptive male partner of a man would have to be lesser, either in age or in status. Same-sex acts between individuals not differentiated by age or status seemed to occur mostly among the less privileged. The comment of John Wilmot, earl of Rochester (1647–80), "missing my whore, I bugger my page," captures the interchangeability of partners from the perspective of the penetrator.[15]

In the casual sexual encounters of elite men, sexual-object choice, that is, the sex of the "chosen" partner, was not really relevant. In 1663 two friends of the English diarist Samuel Pepys, following a long tradition of blaming deviance on foreigners, commented that "buggery is now almost grown as common among our gallants as in Italy." Noting the power differential common to such sexual activities, they added that "the very pages of the town begin to complain of their masters for it."[16] On the one hand, powerful men clearly had access to particularly vulnerable young servants, and the existence of male same-sex sexual activities was no secret. On the other hand, sodomy, defined narrowly as male-male penetration and ejaculation and broadly as any sexual act other than heterosexual vaginal intercourse, was a capital crime. Those convicted might be burned, hanged, or beheaded. Such trials and executions, as well as widely known incidents like those gossiped about by Pepys's cronies that did not lead to prosecution, meant that Europeans were no strangers to same-sex sexuality.

Furthermore, all-male subcultures were known to harbor same-sex sexual activity. Priests (much more rarely nuns) were one group traditionally associated with such relations, but more important in the period of European overseas expansion were pirates and sailors. Aboard ships without women passengers, sexual activity could only be solitary or same-sex. From sodomy trials we have evidence that same-sex activity did take place among both sailors and pirates. Generally these followed the land-dwelling pattern of older and more powerful men initiating sexual relations with younger subordinates. Samuel Norman, a ship's captain, reportedly pulled down the breeches of his fourteen-year-old servant and inserted his "Yard or privity into his Backside." The boy's father complained when they returned to England, but Captain Norman was never brought to trial. Suggesting the tolerance of same-sex sexuality on board ship, numerous witnesses testified that they had seen sixteen-year-old John Durrant and Abdul Rhyme, a Hindu, engaging in sexual activity in a 1649 case. What contributed to the convictions of Durrant and Rhyme was that an English boy had consented to penetration by a "heathen."[17]

There is a lot we do not know about such sexual activities. When were they consensual? It is hard to tell when our primary evidence comes from court trials in which an individual's life might depend on arguing that they were not. Were these simply cases of men, lacking access to women, making do with what they had? Did men inclined to such relations perhaps seek out seafaring occupations?

We know a bit more about those who participated in male urban subcultures that fostered same-sex sexual activity. Such worlds, made possible by concentrations of people, relative anonymity, and independence from the family, began to emerge as early as the fifteenth century in Venice (thus contributing to the notion that sodomy was an "Italian vice"). By the early eighteenth century, when European settler colonies were well established in America, cities such as London, Paris, and Amsterdam sheltered subcultures of effeminate men who frequented taverns, parks, and public latrines, sought out male sexual partners, shared a style of dress and behavior, and could identify each other and be recognized by others outside the subculture. Thus the English Societies for the Reformation of Manners knew where to send their agents in 1707 to entrap men looking for sex, and the patrols of the Parisian police allow us to reconstruct men's cruising routes in the first half of the eighteenth century. Men might signal interest by striking up a conversation or by urinating in front of another man. A French policeman engaged in entrapment reported in 1723 that as he was "about to let flow" in a public park known for cruising, a suspect "asked me what time it was according to my cock and said that according to his it was high noon."[18] Men also gathered in taverns or clubs that tolerated male-male sexual activity. An observer who entered a London club in 1714 found men "calling one another my dear, hugging and kissing, tickling and feeling each other, as if they were a mixture of wanton males and females; and assuming effeminate voice, female airs."[19] Such "sodomites" or, as they were called in England, "mollies"—a term originally applied to female prostitutes—although subject to arrest and punishment, found sexual partners and company within the subculture. That reformers and police knew where to find such men shows that same-sex sexuality was not fully hidden.

Women were noticeably missing from these worlds, but that does not mean that female same-sex sexuality was entirely unknown in European circles. The law, theology, and literature pretty much ignored the possibility of women's having sex with each other, but this was more the result of intentional disbelief than of ignorance. Premodern European culture conceived of women as inherently lustful, but since sex could barely be imagined without a penis, it was not clear what two women could do together besides become aroused in preparation for a man. Nevertheless, some lawmakers considered female same-sex sexuality so detestable and horrible that, as a late fifteenth-century expert put it, it "should not be named or written."[20] Another jurist in the sixteenth century advised the Geneva authorities not to read aloud a description of the crime as was customary in cases of public executions. If word got out, they feared, women, with their weaker natures, might be tempted to seek out such liaisons.

Since women did not have the same possibilities for meeting in public places, it is not surprising that most of the evidence we have comes from cases in which women secretly crossed the gender divide, successfully living as men and marrying women. Whether they did so solely for the economic and social freedom that male dress and employment provided, whether sexual motivation figured into their decisions, or whether they conceived of themselves as transgender people we may never know. In any case, such women fought as soldiers, learned male occupations, met and married women, and came to light only when someone exposed them. Punishment could be swift and severe for the usurpation of male privilege, particularly if it involved the use of what were called "material instruments" to "counterfeit the office of a husband," as a 1566 case put it.[21] In early eighteenth-century Germany, a woman named Catharine Margaretha Linck dressed as a man, served in the army, and, after discharge, went to work as a cotton dyer. He married a woman who, after a quarrel, confessed to her mother that Linck was not what he appeared, prompting the outraged mother to take Linck to court. When the mother produced what another trial transcript in a similar case described as "the illicit inventions she used to supplement the shortcomings of her sex" (in this case fashioned of leather and pigs' bladders), Linck's fate was sealed. She/he was executed in 1721.[22]

Not all women who dressed as men met their doom in this way. Elite women (Queen Christina of Sweden comes to mind), actresses who played "breeches parts," and gangs of women in the underworld sometimes crossed the gender line in relative safety. These last, the "roaring girls" of London or "randy women" of Amsterdam, moved in a world of poverty, petty crime, prostitution, and sexual adventuring. Mary Frith, aka Moll Cutpurse, the model for a "roaring girl" in a number of early seventeenth-century English accounts, struck one fictional observer as "both man and woman," giving her the opportunity to "first cuckold the husband and then make him do as much for the wife."[23] Although we know little about this underworld subculture, the traces it has left in the historical record affirm public knowledge of women's same-sex sexuality.

Accounts of libertines, seafarers, mollies, and roaring girls confirm that the Europeans so shocked by Native American "men/women" in the first century of contact knew more than they let on about same-sex sexuality and the possibility of crossing the gender line.

Out of Africa

Africans, like Europeans, brought complex ideas about sexuality to the New World. And like Native American societies, the West African cultures from which most Africans came exhibited a wide range of sexual practices and attitudes. What is important here is that some fostered greater sexual expressiveness than was characteristic of the dominant European societies, and some institutionalized transgenerational and cross-gender sexuality.

That said, it is true that the sources are relatively silent about same-sex sexuality in Africa. Sixteenth- and seventeenth-century accounts by Europeans mention men dressed as women engaging in sex with other men in Ethiopia, Angola, Madagascar, and elsewhere. Such descriptions echo those of white men in the New World. A history of Ethiopia originally published in 1558 described "passive" men.[24] Antonio Oliveria de Cardonega wrote in his 1681 history of Angola that "there is much sodomy among men, who pursue their dirty practices dressed like women . . . . Some among them are wizzards, who control everything, and are esteemed by most of the people."[25] A 1658 history of Madagascar noted young men who assumed a female role.[26]

In addition, a few societies at different points of African history fostered or tolerated same-sex relations between younger and older partners as part of the socialization process, between adolescent boys in the years before marriage, or between cowives in households where one man married many women. Among the Nzemas of Ghana, "friendship marriage" between a man and a male teenager, and sometimes between two women of different generations, served as a means of transmitting social and spiritual guidance. Among the Azandes of the southern Sudan, chiefs sometimes provided slave girls for their daughters, who would "anoint and paint the girl to make her attractive and then lie with her." Yet Azande men feared sexual relations among their wives, thinking that, as an anthropologist reported, "once a woman has started homosexual intercourse she is likely to continue it because she is then her own master and may have gratification when she pleases and not just when a man cares to give it to her."[27]

What all this meant in the New World remains shrouded in mystery. For most Africans who ended up enslaved, deliberate attempts by white society to break cultural bonds, as well as the conditions of slavery, had an impact on African American sexuality. Not only were Africans torn from their cultures and communities and sometimes deliberately mixed with people from other societies to hinder communication and bonding, but the abolition of the slave trade fostered an emphasis on reproduction and on African American women's sexual availability to men. In the early decades of slavery, the preponderance of male slaves may have fostered same-sex relationships.

That some African Americans engaged in same-sex sexual relations is clear. Jan Creoli, a "negro," was choked to death and his body burned in New Amsterdam in 1646 for committing a second offense of sodomy. The ten-year-old boy, Manuel Congo, "on whom the above abominable crime was committed" was flogged at the place of execution.[28] Some black male slaves in colonial Brazil engaged in sex with each other and with men of Indian and European origins.[29] In both Portugal and Brazil, other African men cross-dressed and probably took a receptive role in sexual encounters with other men.[30] Esteban Montejo, a nineteenth-century Cuban slave who escaped, told in his autobiography of sodomy among plantation slaves that he attributed in part to a shortage of women, but he also noted that some men "did not want to know anything of women." In some cases an effeminate man might take the role of wife to another man, cooking for him and washing the clothes.[31] Although Montejo described the hatred of older slaves for such effeminate men, at the time no pejorative terms existed for same-sex relations.[32]

As the institution of slavery developed, justified by ideas of racial hierarchy, whites' assumptions of sexual excess among black people took root. At the same time, the plantation system promoted sexual violence against both female and male slaves, and sometimes such sexual violence took on a homoerotic tinge. At least since the Crusaders launched their war against Islam and encountered same-sex sexual practices within the Arab and Persian worlds, Europeans had associated sodomy with otherness. So European accounts of same-sex sexuality in Africa, as among the native peoples of the Americas, served as confirmation of the savagery and immorality that justified domination.

As sparse as the evidence is, we know that African Americans came to the New World and survived there with their own sexual systems, based on understandings different from those of their white masters. As both free blacks and enslaved African Americans interacted with their white and sometimes Native American neighbors, a new sexual system came into being.

Sodomiticall Boyes and Lewd Maids

It was of course no equal contest among Native American, European, and African ideas about sexuality. Those who exterminated and enslaved with abandon grabbed the right to decree what was and was not acceptable and "natural" in the realm of sexual behavior. So it comes as no surprise that the colonial societies established in the New World adopted European legal and religious sanctions. Yet America was not Europe. The primitive conditions of the early settlements, the utter lack of anonymity and of urban institutions such as parks and other cruising grounds, the emphasis, especially in New England, on the family, and the necessity for a beleaguered population to reproduce—all of these factors militated against toleration of men with men or women with women.

Yet that did not mean the elimination of all love, desire, and sex between same-sex individuals, as the very prohibitions suggest. Before even touching ground after the arduous trip across the Atlantic, the Reverend Francis Higgeson recorded in 1629 the discovery of "5 beastly Sodomiticall boyes, which confessed their wickedness not to bee named."[33] In the 1650s the Reverend Michael Wigglesworth, a Puritan divine, found himself tormented by "too much doting affection," love, and lust for his Harvard students.[34] In the only known cases concerning women, courts in the Massachusetts Bay Colony found Elizabeth Johnson, a female servant, guilty of "unseemly practices betwixt her and another maid" in 1642. Another court considered the case of two married women, fifteen-year-old Mary Hammon and an older woman, Sara Norman, who engaged in "lewd behavior each with [the] other upon a bed" in 1649. Johnson suffered a severe whipping and paid a fine. Hammon was cleared (perhaps because of her age), and Norman, later accused of "unclean practices" with a man, was let off with a warning.[35] In addition to such acts, we have evidence of at least one woman who crossed the line of gender. During the Revolution, Deborah Sampson disguised herself as a man, joined the Continental army, and romanced other women.

Colonial laws, which singled out male acts, reflected the European condemnation of same-sex sexual relations. Statutes in Plymouth, Massachusetts, Connecticut, and New Hampshire cited as their basis the biblical prohibitions in Leviticus: "If any man lyeth with mankind, as he lyeth with a woman, both of them have committed abomination; they both shall surely be put to death." The Rhode Island law followed the Book of Romans in defining sodomy as "a vile affection, whereby men given up thereto leave the natural use of woman and burn in their lusts one toward another, and so men with men work that which is unseemly." Departing from the general pattern, New Haven outlawed a broad range of sexual acts, including sex between women, anal intercourse between men and women, and sex with children.[36] Jamestown and the other southern colonies adopted the English "buggery" statute of 1533, which called for death for "the horrible, detestable sins of Sodomie."[37]

As the biblical wording of the laws suggests, particularly in New England, religious condemnation of same-sex sexuality thundered from the pulpit. All sex outside marriage merited denunciation. Puritans especially, but most seventeenth-century English Protestants as well, believed that temptation and sin were omnipresent. Faced with so many ways they might depart from the path of the righteous, for them all sexual transgressions, from adultery to sodomy, fell more

Joseph Stone, *Deborah Sampson*, 1797. Oil on panel. RHi(X3) 2513. Courtesy of the Rhode Island Historical Society.

or less in the same category. Yet there were distinctions. Samuel Danforth, in 1673, differentiated "fornication," which included "whoredom," adultery, incest, and "self-pollution," from "going after strange flesh," meaning "filthiness committed by parties of the same sex" and bestiality, or sexual contact with animals.[38] Sodomy and bestiality differed from the other sins because they were unnatural, but like the other sins, they might tempt any individual to commit them. The important point is that engaging in sodomy did not place one in a special category; one was simply a sinner.

Despite the passage of sodomy laws throughout the colonies, regional differences created varying environments for same-sex desire and acts. In the New England colonies, attempts to build model religious communities led to the close supervision of morality in a family-centered world. In the Chesapeake region, in contrast, Europeans came originally to exploit rather than settle, and until the end of the seventeenth century the area contained more men than women, scattered settlements rather than concentrations of population, and more diverse inhabitants, including large numbers of indentured servants and slaves. The sex ratio and the preponderance of young single migrants may have led to more premarital and extramarital sexuality, perhaps including same-sex contacts.

What the legal codes specified and what the ministers preached did not entirely shape people's attitudes toward their neighbors caught in the act. Records document nineteen legal cases involving the charge of sodomy and five executions from 1607 to 1740, although this is no doubt just the tip of the iceberg of actual incidents. Even the minimal evidence we do have suggests that ordinary people, in contrast to the ministers and legislators, did not always harshly judge people accused of same-sex sexuality. Nor did they totally adopt the official perspective on sodomy as an act with no defining consequences for the people involved.

Consider, for instance, the case of Nicholas Sension. A married and prosperous resident of Windsor, Connecticut, in 1677 Sension came before the General Court charged with sodomy. It was not the first complaint against him. Thirty years earlier, and then again in the 1660s, relatives of young men whom he had accosted had complained to the authorities, who merely reprimanded him. In the 1677 trial, witness after witness testified to Sension's often violent sexual advances: "He took me and threw me on the chest, and took hold of my privy parts . . . . the said Sension came to me with his yard or member erected in his hands, and desired me to lie on my belly, and strove with me."[39] Over the years, Sension had sought sex from a number of young men, many of them servants, but he had most recently fixed his attention on a young retainer in his household, Nathaniel Pond. Pond had confided in his brother about his master's "grossly lascivious carriages toward him," complaining that he "did often in an unseemly manner make attempts tending to sodomy." Witnesses told of seeing Sension in the servants' sleeping quarters at night, on one occasion trying to fondle the slumbering Pond. Sension desisted only when Pond's bed partner awoke—people at this time routinely slept with others without any sexual connotations. Because only one witness claimed that Sension had succeeded in committing sodomy and the law required two, the court found Sension guilty of attempted sodomy, placing his estate in bond for his good behavior but ordering no other financial or corporal penalty.

What does it mean that the good citizens of Windsor tolerated Sension's behavior for decades and the court, when called to judge him, merely slapped him on the wrist? Reactions to Sension give no indication of the horror and disgust reflected in the legal and religious pronouncements. It is true that not all accused men escaped so lightly. William Plaine of New Haven was put to death in 1646 for committing "sodomy with two persons in England" and for having "corrupted a great part of the youth of Guilford by masturbations, which he had committed, and provoked others to the like above a hundred times." And the same court sentenced John Knight to death in 1655 for attempting sodomy on a teenage boy after he had already been convicted for sexually abusing a child.

But even if Sension's case is unusual because of his standing in the community, the glimpse it affords us of popular responses and one man's self-perception is invaluable. That Sension's pursuit of young men was widely known and little acted on suggests some ambivalence about the "crime" of sodomy. Nathaniel Pond himself, toward whom Sension expressed "fond affection," refused Sension's offer of a release from his indenture, saying he was "loathe to leave him who had the trouble of his education in his minority." Although Sension's pursuit of younger and subordinate men fit the traditional European pattern, a neighbor testified that Sension admitted that he had "long" practiced "this trade," the very term suggesting a preference and a way of life.

The same understanding emerges from the trial of Stephen Gorton, a married Baptist minister in New London, also accused over a thirty-year period of "unchaste behaviour with his fellow men when in bed with them." In 1757 the church decreed that his "offensive and unchaste behaviour, frequently repeated for a long space of time," gave evidence of "an inward disposition . . . towards the actual commission of a sin of so black and dark a dye." Despite this judgment, Gorton won reinstatement to his position after confessing his sins. Gorton's "inward disposition," like Sension's "trade," hints at a concept that sat uneasily with the official definition of sodomy as a horrific act that any sinner might commit, but not one that defined the sinner as a special kind of person.

A very different kind of case, played out in Warrosquyoacke, Virginia, in 1629, supports the notion that ordinary people might hold different views than the religious and legal authorities.[40] Here the issue was not sodomy but gender transgression. A servant, sometimes known as Thomas and other times as Thomasine Hall, raised such confusion in the minds of the community that groups of both women and men felt compelled to find out the nature of his/her genitalia. Hall had been raised in England as a girl but at the age of twenty-four "Cut of[f] his heire and Changed his apparell into the fashion of man" and joined the army.[41] Upon returning from service in France, Hall changed back into a woman and worked as a seamstress. Deciding to emigrate to Virginia in 1627, he boarded ship as a man. Apparently once settled in Virginia as a servant, Hall sometimes dressed as a woman and employed "feminine" skills in needlework. Hall claimed to be both a man and a woman.

In attempting to determine Hall's "true" gender, community matrons, Hall's master, and the authorities all took different approaches. Several times groups of women—as was customary in cases of witchcraft or premarital pregnancy—searched Hall's body to see what they would find. That they did so suggests they must have assumed she was female, for they would not have presumed to examine a male body. In the women's eyes Hall's anatomy clinched it—he had what he himself described as "a peece of flesh growing at the . . . belly as bigg as the topp of his little finger [an] inch long," although "hee had not the use of the man's p[ar]te."[42] With such a penis, if ever so small and nonfunctional, he must be a man. Yet Hall's original Virginia master and the first local authority to undertake an examination of Hall both concluded she was a woman. Likewise, Hall's second master at first insisted that an individual without male sexual functions who sometimes dressed as a woman had to be female. He changed his mind only when, called by the female searchers to witness what they had found, he looked in vain for the "peece of an hole"

Hall claimed to have.[43] Without a vagina, he could not be a woman, so the master decided that Hall should dress as a man after all. A while later, dressed in male clothing, Hall met two men who threw him down to see whether he was male or female; Hall "pulled out his members whereby it appeared," according to the men who later testified about the event, "that hee was a p[er]fect man."[44]

Given such uncertainty about Hall's sex and gender and the nature of his/her transgression, the community passed the case to the Jamestown General Court, where Hall told her/his story. Given the conflicting testimony and the history of changeability, the court ordered Hall to wear men's breeches but a woman's apron and cap.

The community seemed most concerned about deciding what clothes Hall should wear to inform others of his/her gender. Yet gender confusion always carried the possibility of inappropriate same-sex sexual acts. In Hall's case, the question of sexuality arose only when a rumor spread that he/she had engaged in a tryst with a maidservant. But another exchange reported in court is intriguing. A witness testified that a man had asked Hall why he wore women's clothing, and Hall had replied, "I goe in weomans aparell to gett a bitt for my Catt."[45] What did this mean? There's no way to know for sure, but it might have been a sly English translation of a then current French slang expression (remember Thomas's military service in France), "pour avoir une bit pour mon chat" or "to get a prick for my cunt."[46] In other words, she wanted to appear as a woman in order to attract a male sexual partner.

Whatever Hall's sexual desires, the case reveals conflicting understandings of gender and the lack of a distinct category for transgendered individuals such as existed in Native American and some African societies. Hall him/herself preferred the freedom to switch between male and female; the women and

Hall's master sought to fix his/her gender based on bodily characteristics; others involved in the case accepted Hall as a woman because of her feminine skills and mannerisms; the court ordered a mixed presentation that shamed Hall as a man and limited her/his ability to move across the boundaries of gender.

What the cases of Nicholas Sension and Thomas/Thomasine Hall show is that colonial attitudes toward gender and sexual transgression were complex, shaped not only by European law, custom, and religious dictates but also by the active participation of the community. Religious and civil authorities focused on the sinful unnatural acts, which they placed in the same category as other deviant sexual behavior. There was no permanent cultural category or identity for those who engaged in same-sex sexual relations or for those who could not easily be labeled male or female. Nevertheless, evidence does suggest a popular perception that some individuals regularly engaged in—and preferred—same-sex sexual behavior, and that some individuals bridged the cultural categories of man and woman. Law, religion, and the everyday perspectives of ordinary people—as well as the alternative possibilities for sexuality and gender embodied in Native American and African sexual systems—all went into the fashioning of a New World sexuality.

By the time of the Revolution, the new Americans who made the laws had hammered out understandings of gender and sexual morality that contrasted markedly with those of Native American and African societies. But despite European blindness to anything other than a two-category system of "men" and "women," a case such as that of Thomas/Thomasine Hall forced them to confront a murkier reality. Likewise Deborah Sampson's excursions across the gender line, in the tradition of cross-dressing women in the European past, showed that "female men" were found not only in Native American and African cultures.

In the same way, the story of Nicholas Sension's neighbors and the Reverend Mr. Gorton's parishioners reveals that the windows of tolerance for same-sex sexuality that we find in some African and Native American societies might have also existed, albeit in different form, among the Europeans in America. Perhaps the libertine tradition accustomed them to accept Sension's assaults as long as he adhered to the status hierarchy. Certainly their not fully articulated notion of Sension's "trade" and Gorton's "disposition" reminds us that we need to know more than what the legal and religious authorities said about same-sex sexuality. What people desired, what they did, and what they thought were part of the complex process of building a sexual system.

Three

WORLDS OF MEN, WORLDS OF WOMEN:
SEX AND ROMANTIC FRIENDSHIP IN AN
INDUSTRIALIZING AND EXPANDING
NATION

In 1975, while married to a man, I fell in love with a woman. In the early stages my new relationship was purely romantic. I thought about her all the time, we talked endlessly on the telephone, I gave her presents, I longed to be with her. The way the three of us understood what was going on was that she was "really" heterosexual and had just happened to fall in love with me, while I was "really" a lesbian and in the process of coming out. And then I read Carroll Smith-Rosenberg's eye-opening article titled "The Female World of Love and Ritual: Relations between Women in Nineteenth-Century America."[1]

I devoured the story of Molly Hallock Foote and her friend Helena, who met in school in New York in 1868. In an early letter to Helena, Molly wrote, "I have not said to you in so many or so few words that I was happy with you during those few so incredibly short weeks but surely you do not need words to tell you what you must know. Those two or three days so dark without, so bright with firelight and contentment within I shall always remember as proof that, for a time, at least—I fancy for quite a long time—we might be sufficient for each other . . . . Imagine yourself kissed many times by one who loved you so dearly." As their friendship deepened, they made plans to live together. Molly pledged her love: "I wanted so to put my arms round my girl of all the girls in the world and tell her . . . I love her as wives do love their husbands, as *friends* who have taken each other for life." But shortly thereafter Helena decided to marry, and Molly followed suit two years later. In the interval between their marriages, Molly confided, "You know dear Helena, I really was in love with you. It was a passion such as I had never known until I saw you." And to Helena's fiancé, in a letter of congratulations, Molly wrote bluntly, "Do you know sir, that until you came along I believe that she loved me almost as girls love their lovers. *I know I loved her so.* Don't you wonder that I can stand the sight of you."[2]

And this was only one of dozens of examples of passionate, intense, loving, physically affectionate relationships— what have come to be called "romantic friendships"—that Smith-Rosenberg had uncovered in the correspondence of a wide range of American middle-class families between the 1760s and the 1880s. Perhaps most amazing, as Molly's forthrightness in addressing Helena's fiancé suggests, such friendships were widely accepted, even admired, and often lasted from adolescence through marriage and into old age. Smith-Rosenberg concluded that the supposedly repressive Victorian sexual system in fact allowed far more latitude in moving along a spectrum ranging from what we would call heterosexuality to homosexuality than does late twentieth-century American society.

Now let me try to reconstruct for a moment what this article meant to me. It was not that it was all right to be a lesbian because there had been lesbians in the past. Nor was it that what I was feeling was all right because it was not "homosexuality." Rather, it was that our modern categories of heterosexuality and homosexuality (and even bisexuality) are not complex enough to capture the slippery reality of love and desire. I seized upon this article because Smith-Rosenberg's vision of a world in which love and sexuality had no easy relation to sexual identity made sense to me, unsure as I was if I yet merited the label "lesbian." And though the woman I fell in love with is now married to a man and I happily identify as a lesbian, I do not take that to mean those were the only possible outcomes.

The historical phenomenon of romantic friendship suggests how different the world of the late eighteenth and nineteenth centuries was from colonial society, where two women might commit "unseemly practices" and engage in "lewd behavior." To say nothing of the late twentieth century! The strangeness of romantic friendship to our modern eyes leads us to pause for a moment to consider why sexuality is so differently understood at different points in time. The nineteenth century witnessed great commercial and industrial growth in the North, political upheaval and the end of slavery in the South, and the movement of different groups of the population into new territories, all developments that had a profound impact on sexuality. So, after considering the changing sexual system, I turn to different forms of same-sex love and sexuality. We find both the newer relationship of romantic friendship and the persistence of older patterns of interaction: sexual behavior within sex-segregated subcultures and men and women crossing the gender line. And we see the beginnings of urban worlds in which men who loved men might find each other.

A Transformed Sexual System

What I have been calling the "sexual system" is closely connected to large-scale economic, social, and political developments. Although in everyday life we tend to think of sexuality as something personal, historians of sexuality see it as a complex product of individual desires, group activities and ideas, and societal forces. As the country grew up, the ways people expressed their love and desire changed.

How, exactly, did this happen? One key is that the family became less central as an economic unit. The rise of factory production in the Northeast accelerated the process, already under way with the growth of commercialized agriculture and the expansion of trade, of moving the production of goods and services away from the farmstead. Wage labor made a stark distinction between those who earned money and those who did not. Children not employed as laborers became less of an economic asset and required more of a financial investment. So white, American-born, urban middle-class families began to have fewer children, making use of contraception and abortion as well as abstinence from sexual intercourse to limit family size. In such a context, guardians of sexual morality could less easily proclaim reproduction the sole purpose of sexuality, eliminating one argument against nonreproductive sexual acts, including those engaged in by same-sex partners. Although the birthrate decline was not universal (African American slave women, southern white women, white women on the frontier of white settlement, and immigrant women continued to bear large numbers of children), the trend begun in the middle and upper classes in the urban Northeast spread throughout society.

As productive activities such as weaving cloth and making shoes moved outside the household, some women followed them into the factory while others, whose families could afford it, stayed at home. Despite the reality of "factory girls," women engaged in agricultural labor, and women who continued to do work such as spinning and weaving at home as part of the "putting out" system of production, societal norms increasingly emphasized the domestic roles of women. Associating women with the home and men with the world outside, the dominant ideology posited a fundamental difference between men and women and between male and female sexuality. The double standard was nothing new, but traditionally women in Western society had been viewed as just as sexual as men—or even more so. The nineteenth-century sexual system, which continues to undergird our contemporary assumptions that men are more interested in sex than women are, reversed the older ideas about female lasciviousness and proclaimed the ideal woman inherently passionless. As a response to the increasing separation of male and female spheres of activity among the urban middle class, the tenet of women's sexual difference from men served to aid middle-class men's sexual self-control within marriage. Ironically, the ideology of profound sexual difference, in conjunction with economic and social sex segregation, also encouraged same-sex love and sexuality.

And finally, differences of race and class, as well as gender, intensified in the nineteenth century, with consequences for the history of same-sex sexuality. As the nation expanded in the course of the century, not only did whites and African Americans move west into Indian territory, but Mexicans moved north and Chinese and Japanese immigrants moved east, leading to all sorts of interactions across the lines of ethnicity. Sexuality, and lack of sexual self-control, became increasingly associated, in the eyes of the white middle class, with racial and ethnic minorities and the working class.

This was so partly because not all groups conformed to the dominant sexual system, leading its proponents to label them immoral. African American slave communities, for example, maintained their own values with regard to courtship, sexuality, marriage, childbearing, and divorce. Mexican women and men on the southwestern frontier, in accordance with a Mexican working-class custom, accepted cohabitation in informal unions as well as marriage. And people in urban working-class neighborhoods, where sex had always been more public than in middle- and upper-class districts, lived among the burgeoning dance halls, taverns, and other institutions that fostered a sexualized commercial culture. As men of all classes moved freely in the booming sexual underworlds, young, single, working-class women in urban areas began to challenge both older conceptions of their depravity and new ones of their asexuality to carve out a culture that had some chance of meeting their own sexual and emotional needs.

An intriguing tidbit in the records of slaveowners who claimed compensation for their loss of "property" when slaves ran off to the British in the War of 1812 illustrates the importance of race in understanding sexuality. In 1828 a witness supporting a white woman's claim for compensation described a slave woman, Minty, as having two surnames, Gurry and Caden. The first was that of her husband, from whom she had parted shortly after their marriage. She then "formed an intimacy with a negro woman" and took her name. This tantalizing fragment suggests both the possibility that slave cultures recognized same-sex ties and that slaveowners might matter-of-factly report the existence of such relationships.[3]

The association of sexuality with race and class both fostered intimate (but presumably nonsexual) same-sex relations among the middle class and eroticized cross-class and interracial relations. Labeling working-class people and people of color as more sexual also justified the existence of prostitution and the sexual exploitation of women of color and working-class women by elite white men.

The separation of sexuality and reproduction, the assertion of female and male difference, and the increased
differentiation of sexuality along lines of gender, race, and
class had important consequences for the expression of same-
sex desire. As cities grew, as waves of immigrants landed on
American shores, as factories belched their fumes above the
landscape, as African Americans celebrated their freedom, as
people trekked west, east, and north, the old order gave way.

Romantic Friendship

In the settled Northeast, the ideology of sexual difference
between women and men flourished among the urban middle
class. If women's and men's polarized natures were, in theory,
intended to combine in marriage, they also quite logically led
to the glorification of same-sex relations. Marriage might rep-
resent the union of two unlike halves, but intense, passionate
relationships between two similar souls thrived in addition to
and, for women, alongside marriage.

We have already witnessed the intensity of Molly and
Helena's love. Although the fierceness of Molly's attachment
and the destructiveness of marriage to their bond might set
them apart from other romantic friends, their expressions
of love and physical affection did not. Consider the saga
of fourteen-year-old Sarah Butler Wister and sixteen-year-
old Jeannie Field Musgrove, who met in the summer of
1849. Their friendship deepened during two years together
in boarding school, where Sarah adorned Jeannie's portrait
with a bouquet of flowers and took on a male nom de plume.
Their relationship continued right through marriage and into
old age. As a twenty-nine-year-old mother, Sarah wrote to her
beloved Jeannie, "I can give you no idea how desperately I shall
want you." After visits together, Jeannie wrote, "Dear darling
Sarah! How I love you & how happy I have been! You are

the joy of my life." And "I want you to tell me in your next letter, to assure me, that I am your dearest . . . . So just fill a quarter page with caresses & expressions of endearment." Jeannie addressed Sarah as "my dearest, dearest lover" and sent "a thousand kisses." When Jeannie married at the ripe old age of thirty-seven, Sarah wrote from afar, "I have thought & thought & yearned over you these two days . . . . My dearest love to you wherever and *who*ever you are."[4]

What is remarkable in this relationship—the intensity and the longevity—is typical of romantic friendships among women. The poet Emily Dickinson fell in love with her friend Sue Gilbert, who later married Dickinson's brother. In 1852 Dickinson wrote to Gilbert: "Susie, will you indeed come home next Saturday, and be my own again, and kiss me as you used to? . . . I hope for you so much, and feel so eager for you, feel that I *cannot* wait, feel that *now* I must have you—that the expectation once more to see your face again, makes me feel hot and feverish, and my heart beats so fast."[5] In 1808 Sarah Foulke wrote in her diary, "I laid with my dear R[ebecca] and a glorious good talk we had until about 4[A.M.]—O how hard I do *love* her." Eunice Callender carved her and Sarah Ripley's initials into a tree, with a pledge of eternal love. Eliza Schlatter wrote to her friend Sophie DuPont in 1834, "I wish I could be with you present in the body as well as the mind & heart—I would turn your *good husband out of bed*—and snuggle into you and we would have a long talk like old times."[6]

Surviving letters between two white Georgia women, Alice Baldy and Josie Varner, suggest that southern women too formed romantic friendships, although these likely differed from those of women in the more urban and industrial region of the country.[7] Like many of their northern counterparts, Baldy and Varner met in college in the 1850s. Baldy, from a once-wealthy family that had run into hard times in the 1860s, scraped out a living as a teacher. She dreamed of running a school with Varner, who worked in her family's hotel, but this was never to be. Baldy wrote Varner in 1870: "I am only a woman like yourself, yet you never had, & never can have a more devoted, sincere & constant lover than you have in me; and mine, my dear, is a love that will never tire."[8] And later that same year:

Do you know that if you only touch me, or speak to me there is not a nerve or fibre in my body that does not respond with a thrill of delight? . . . You remember the morning you came in the parlor . . . and, taking my head in your arms, you bent down with *such* a smile & *such* a look! and gave me the sweetest kiss any body could imagine . . . I was quite happy.[9]

But perhaps because Varner did not reciprocate Baldy's love with the same intensity, the two women lived out their lives apart, Baldy struggling to make ends meet.

As these stories make clear, romantic friendships among women grew out of a female world of kin and friends bound together by female-controlled rituals, such as birth, marriage, and death, and institutions such as boarding schools or colleges and the custom of "visiting." Women met their lifelong friends through their families or at school, and they often maintained an intimate friendship into marriage. Until the opening of employment, especially in the professions, provided the prospect of economic independence for middle-class women, marriage seemed the only possibility. Unmarried daughters had little choice except to remain within the family, moving to the household of a brother or sister after their parents' deaths. By the second half of the nineteenth century, however, the expansion of employment opportunities meant that romantic friends might decide to forgo marriage and make a life together. These partnerships between romantic friends, which became known as "Boston marriages" because of their prevalence in the older cities, substituted for heterosexual marriage in a way that ultimately proved threatening to the social order.

But until the late nineteenth century, romantic friendships among women could meet with not just toleration but approbation, as long as they did not in some way cross the lines of respectability. Prescriptive literature advocated such bonds as particularly appropriate for women, who were thought to be emotional, spiritual creatures with little to do in the world. Assumptions about women's asexuality help explain society's acceptance of what might look to modern eyes like lesbian relationships. If women and men (or at least white middle-class women and men) were conceptualized as polar opposites—men represented by the head and hand and women by the heart, men inherently lustful and women naturally pure and without desire—then what could be more natural than that women would find their soulmates among each other and that society would condone this?

What is harder to understand is society's acceptance of a more limited form of romantic friendship among young men. Listen to the story of Albert Dodd and Anthony Halsey, college students in the 1830s, who loved each other and slept together in the same bed. Albert, in his journal, referred to his "adored Anthony," "my most beloved of all," and described his friend as "so handsome." "Often too," he wrote, Anthony "shared my pillow—or I his, and then how sweet to sleep with him, to hold his beloved form in my embrace, to have his arms about my neck, to imprint upon his face sweet kisses."[10]

Or what about Daniel Webster and James Hervey Bingham, who formed a warm friendship at Dartmouth, then studied law, taught school, and served as law clerks together? In letters they addressed each other as "Lovely Boy" or "Dearly Beloved." Daniel described "dear Hervey" as "the only friend of my heart, the partner of my joys, griefs, and affections, the only participator of my most secret thoughts." "I don't see how I can live any longer without having a friend near me, I mean a male friend, just such a friend as one J. H. B.," he lamented. Then he announced that he would move in: "Yes, James, I must come; we will yoke together again; your little bed is just wide enough; we will practise at the same bar, and be as friendly a pair of single fellows as ever cracked a nut."[11]

In the years before the Civil War, intellectuals and artists associated with the transcendentalist movement spread word of romantic friendships among men as well as women. Ralph Waldo Emerson wrote an essay titled "On Friendship," and Herman Melville, whose *Moby Dick* explores the intense relationships of men at sea, dedicated his masterpiece to his friend and fellow artist Nathaniel Hawthorne.[12] In the novel, when the hero Ishmael first meets Queequeg, the harpooner from the South Seas, it is as his unknown bedmate in an inn. "Upon waking next morning about daylight, I found Queequeg's arm thrown over me in the most loving and affectionate manner. You had almost thought I had been his wife." And the next night, having gotten to know Queequeg and having "felt a melting in me," Ishmael comments: "How it is I know not; but there is no place like a bed for confidential disclosures between friends. Man and wife, they say, there open the very bottom of their souls to each other; and some old couples often lie and chat over old times till nearly morning. Thus, then, in our hearts' honeymoon, lay I and Queequeg—a cosy, loving pair."[13]

This sounds, of course, a great deal like the romantic friendship that flourished among women. But there was one big difference: however much these young men might long to live together, society expected their friendships to change with adulthood and marriage, because success in the middle-class male professional and business worlds called for a competitive spirit quite at odds with such youthful devotion. Although male romantic friends shared the female ones' sense that only same-sex friends could truly understand one another, they differed in the loosening of these bonds after the period of youth, at least if they married. Like women, young men formed ardent and romantic attachments and engaged in touching, kissing, and caressing. But they were expected to move beyond such intense attachment when they became adults and married.

Kissing, hugging, even sharing a bed, which was commonplace, as we have seen, could be done openly, with no self-consciousness, because these were expressions of emotional intimacy, not sexuality. The revelation that Abraham Lincoln shared a double bed (and his most private thoughts) for almost four years with general store proprietor Joshua Speed as he started out on his illustrious career in Springfield, Illinois, has attracted a great deal of attention, leading on the one hand to claims that this means he was "gay" and on the other to attempts to use this piece of history to raise awareness of the different ways that male intimacy could be expressed in the past.[14]

By the end of the nineteenth century, physical affection between men began to take on a different coloration. Frederick S. Ryman, a New Yorker who in 1886 recorded in his diary his fondness for "the Oriental custom of men embracing & kissing each other" and described sleeping with his friend Rob's arms around him, drew a clear line between such cuddling and heterosexual intercourse. "I am certain there was no sexual sentiment on the part of either of us. We both have our mistresses . . . & I am certain that the thought of the least demonstration of unmanly & abnormal passion would have been as revolting to him as it is & ever has been to me."[15] If perhaps he protested too much for us to believe that he experienced no "abnormal passions," he had certainly learned his lines. If not all men in fact forgot their male friends in the interests of marriage and manhood (the poet Walt

Male friends relax together, a turn-of-the-century cabinet
card. Courtesy of Seekers Antiques, Columbus, Ohio.

Whitman and Mormon luminary Evan Stephens, as we shall see, maintained their passionate male friendships into old age) the persistence of such attachments began to shade into more questionable behavior.

For both women and men of the middle class, romantic friendship represented an emotional and sensual option. Society's acceptance of such bonds, and their compatibility with cross-sex relationships, reveals a conception of the nature of sexuality that differs from what had gone before and what would come after. Acts that would later be construed as sexual could be engaged in unself-consciously, not only by women assumed to be passionless but also by young men. This was to some extent (though not entirely) a class-bound form of relationship. The extended youth of middle-class men and the leisure of middle-class women played a central role in shaping romantic friendship, while the association of sexuality with the working class preserved the presumed asexuality of these relations.

It would be a mistake, however, to assume that the social acceptance of romantic friendship means that sexual acts never occurred between romantic friends. The 1826 letters of Thomas Jefferson Withers to James H. Hammond—who both went on to become southern pro-slavery and states' rights advocates—reveal a forthright eroticism that seems at odds with the chaste youthful bed sharing associated with male romantic friendship. "I feel some inclination to learn whether you yet sleep in your Shirt-tail," the twenty-two-year-old Withers wrote, "and whether you yet have the extravagant delight of poking and punching a writhing Bedfellow with your long fleshen pole—the exquisite touches of which I have often had the honor of feeling? . . . Sir, you roughen the downy Slumbers of your Bedfellow—by such hostile—furious lunges as you are in the habit of making at him—when he is least prepared for defence against the crushing force of a Battering Ram."[16] Perhaps such a nonfurtive and playful description of male same-sex sexuality reflects the lingering influence of the male libertine tradition in the United States South. Perhaps in the tradition of boys' boarding schools, same-sex sexuality was a common but little-discussed part of adolescence. Or perhaps the letters expose an elaborate jest. In any case, the Withers-Hammond letters throw into question the innocence of male love in the ninetenth century.

What about women? It perhaps comes as no surprise that some men might have engaged in sexual acts, for men's lusts were legendary. Quite a different example shows that women might have engaged in, and interpreted in different ways, acts that seem quite sexual to modern eyes. Two African American women, freeborn domestic servant Addie Brown and schoolteacher Rebecca Primus, forged a passionate relationship in Hartford, Connecticut, in the 1860s. Across the chasm of class, eighteen-year-old Addie somehow met Rebecca, five years older, well-respected, and politically committed, as evinced by her journey south to teach freed slaves in Maryland. That they identified with the model of white women's romantic friendship is suggested by Addie's commentary on Grace Aguilar's 1850 book *Women's Friendships,* the tale of a friendship between an aristocratic and a middle-class British woman. Yet as Addie put it, "You have been more to me then a *friend* or *sister.*" When apart, Addie brooded. "Rebecca, when I bid you good by it's seem to me that my very heart broke . . . . My Darling Friend I shall never be happy again unless I am near you eather here on earth or in heaven . . . . I will always love you and you only."[17]

That their relationship involved at the very least the touching of breasts is revealed by a letter Addie wrote from her post at Miss Porter's School, where she reported that the "girls are very friendly towards me . . . . One of them wants to sleep with me. Perhaps I will give my consent some of these nights." In response to Rebecca's (lost) reply, Addie explained: "If you think that is my bosom that captivated the girl that made her want to sleep with me, she got sadly disappointed injoying it, for I had my back towards all night and my night dress *was* butten up so she could not get to my bosom. I shall try to keep your f[avored] one always for you. Should in my excitement forget, you will partdon me *I know*."[18]

Addie did not categorize her feelings for Rebecca as utterly different from her attraction to men. She wrote that she preferred Rebecca's kisses to those of the African American head of the household where she worked as a servant. "How I did miss you last night. I did not have anyone to hug me up and to kiss . . . . I don't want anyone to kiss me now. I turn Mr. Games away this morning. No *kisses* is like youres." And "You are the first girl that I ever *love* so and you are the *last* one . . . . If you was a man, what would things come to? They would after come to something very quick." "What a pleasure it would be to me to address you *My Husband*."[19]

Not only did the two women share love and erotic passion, but their relationship merited recognition in their community. While Rebecca was teaching in the South, her mother defended their relationship. As Addie reported, "She said I thought as much of you if you was a gentleman. She also said if either one of us was a gent we would marry."[20] In a sense, the bond between the two women fit the pattern of extending kin ties to nonfamily members that was typical in both slave and free African American communities. Yet there were limits. Rebecca's aunt warned Addie not to let her suitor, Joseph Tines, know of the depth of her love for Rebecca: "She also said if Mr. T[ines] was to see me, think that I care more for you then I did for him. I told, I did love you more then I ever would him. She said I better not tell him so."[21]

What Addie really wanted was to live with Rebecca. "Rebecca, if I could live with you or even be with you some parts of the day, I would never marry."[22] But it was not to be. With great ambivalence, Addie married her suitor, stopped her correspondence with Rebecca, and died of tuberculosis at age twenty-nine. Rebecca also married and lived to be ninety-five.

It is impossible to know how widespread such relationships might have been in the African American community or whether the caressing of breasts Addie and Rebecca seemed to engage in was part of more romantic friendships than we know. What these rich letters do suggest, though—along with the briefer Hammond-Withers correspondence—is that romantic friendship was a complex experience that could take many forms. Some women, like Addie Brown and Rebecca Primus, may have acted on their erotic desires. Perhaps others did not, or found satisfaction in the kissing, caressing, and fondling of ordinary romantic friendship. As long as they did not cross the lines of respectability in some way—by appearing "mannish" or utterly rejecting men, as Rebecca's aunt warned Addie not to do—romantic friends may have had quite a lot of leeway to express their love and desire.

Cowboys, Miners, Mormons, and Prostitutes: Sex in Single-Sex Communities

As urbanization and industrialization swept across the Northeast, quite a different story unfolded on the frontiers where migrants encountered new worlds. From the East and South, individuals and families undertook the journey farther and farther west into territories populated by Native Americans, where they reestablished a preindustrial mode of economic organization. At the same time, they took with them the ideas of their previous worlds, including the notion of appropriate male and female spheres. But the boomtowns of the frontier were not New York or Boston. For one thing, far more men than women went to make their fortunes in mining or ranching. The scarcity of women meant the creation of all-male worlds. For women the sex imbalance led to a variety of sexual alternatives to traditional monogamous marriage, some voluntary and some forced: polygyny in the case of the Mormons, cohabitation for Mexican women, sexual slavery for Chinese women, and sexual exploitation or prostitution for some women of all groups. For cowboys, miners, and prostitutes, life on the frontier brought increased sex segregation. Although evidence is scarce, those subcultures seem to have fostered same-sex sexual relations.

An early frontier of white settlement gave rise to the popular stories about Davy Crockett, the mythic hero of the Tennessee wilderness. From the 1830s to the 1850s, readers across the country devoured the tall tales in which Crockett battled nature, killed Indians with his bare hands, and subdued wild animals. Although the stories gave Crockett a wife and daughters, he moved in a savage and largely male world where his domination of both animals and other men took on a cast of same-sex sexuality. Consider an 1846 account, for example, of Crockett's taming a wild stallion:

I grabbed him by the scuff of the mane, jerked him down instantly and mounted him slick as a cow bird on the back of a brindle bull. I then locked my feet under him . . . and off we put . . . the tarnal critter tried to . . . brush me off, but I pull his head . . . give him a kick in the flank . . . . After that he laid right down and grunted the perfect cart-horse submission an tameness.

Or this 1836 tale of a fight with a stagecoach driver:

I jumped right down upon the driver and he tore my trowsers right off me . . . . luckily there was a poker in the fire which I thrust down his throat, and by that means mastered him.[23]

As with pirates and sailors in earlier times, same-sex sexuality among groups of men on the frontier seems to have been a response to isolation from women and perhaps in some cases what drew men to frontier living—or at least did not deter them. Cowboys and miners spent most of their time in all-male company. Their work was hard and their culture unrelentingly masculine, and they developed special rituals. When cowboys castrated bulls, for example, they cooked and ate the testicles.[24] Although both miners and cowboys caroused with available women when they had the chance, some also took on "female" roles as dance partners when no women were available. A 1922 western novel described a raucous all-male dance in a mining camp: "A roar of laughter came from the celebrating miners and all eyes turned their way. Sinful and Hank were dancing to the music of a jew's-harp and the time set by stamping, hob-nailed boots. They parted, bowed, joined again, parted, curtsied and went on, hand in hand, turning and ducking, backing and filing, the dust flying and the perspiration streaming down."[25]

Some cowboys paired off and formed deep attachments with their sidekicks. A ranch hand who had worked in South Dakota and Arizona wrote a poem after his partner's death, describing his feelings that "Al ain't here no more!" Published in 1915, the poem included these lines:

> We loved each other in the way men do
> And never spoke about it, Al and me.
> But we both *knowed,* and knowin' it so true
> Was more than any woman's kiss could be.
> . . . .
> I wait to hear him ridin' up behind And feel his knee rub
> mine the good old way.[26]

North of the United States border, in British Columbia, similar lifelong bonds between men in the nineteenth century led one gold miner to commit suicide after the death of a partner, leaving a note that read, "I can't live without Cy."[27]

That cowboy life might also lead to sexual relations is suggested by the testimony of early twentieth-century cowboys.
One Oklahoma cowboy described the sexual progression of
cowboy partners: "At first pairing they'd solace each other
gingerly and, as bashfulness waned, manually. As trust in
mutual good will matured, they'd graduate to the ecstatically
comforting . . . . Folk know not how cock-hungry men get."
Bonding, he wrote, "was at first rooted in admiration, infat-
uation, a sensed need of an ally, loneliness and yearning, but
it regularly ripened into love."[28] Another man who worked
in logging and gold mining camps in the early years of the
twentieth century also reported widespread sexual activity.[29]

Furthermore, off-color cowboy limericks reinforce the
notion that cowboy culture could foster same-sex relations.
Listen to these two examples:

> There was a cowboy named Hooter,
> Who packed a big six-shooter,
> When he grabbed the stock
> It became hard as a rock,
> As a peace-maker it couldn't be cuter.

> Young cowboys had a great fear,
> That old studs once filled with beer,
> Completely addle'
> They'd throw on a saddle,
> And ride them on the rear.[30]

The same kinds of attachments may have formed among
other groups of men on the frontier. Cowboys and miners
came from a variety of cultures, including Mexican, African
American, and Chinese, in which same-sex relations were traditionally viewed differently than in European American society. In Mexico the most important distinction was between
"active" and "passive" sexual acts among men; as in the older

European libertine tradition, to penetrate was acceptable, to be penetrated was not. In China, same-sex relations between men who also married women had a long tradition. Two terms for male love—"the love of shared peach" and "the cut sleeve"—derive from ancient stories about elite men. In the first case a peach proved so delicious that a man offered the rest of it to his ruler, whom he held in great affection. In the other an emperor and his lover fell asleep one afternoon, the lover's head on the emperor's sleeve; when the ruler had to attend to business, he cut off his sleeve rather than disturb his lover.[31] Although the Qing dynasty in the mid-eighteenth century cracked down on the blossoming of male love, it is possible that male same-sex sexuality flourished in Chinese enclaves in the United States. Certainly the distorted sex ratio among the Chinese population, the result of deliberate immigration policies designed to prevent family settlement, militated in that direction. In California in 1860, for example, there were almost twenty Chinese men for every Chinese woman, most of whom were brought into the country to work as pros-titutes. Male same-sex sexuality may have bloomed within the Chinese bachelor societies that formed in the early years of settlement. We do know that labor contractors provided male prostitutes for Pacific Coast Asian American cannery workers in the 1920s and 1930s, confirming the existence of same-sex sexuality among the Chinese, Japanese, and Filipino workers.[32] Just as different sexual systems came into play in the early years of European settlement, so too on the frontier did different cultures interact.

Within the Mormon community of Salt Lake City—yet another distinct culture on the frontier of white western settlement—same-sex relationships took on various forms. Despite the family basis of Mormon migration and settle-ment, Mormon congregations remained segregated by gen-der throughout most of the nineteenth century, encouraging same-sex love and intimacy. Male Mormon missionaries, even when married, often left their wives for two years or more to spread the word of God. The church directed such men to be celibate and to remain glued to the side of a missionary companion in order to ward off loneliness. A guide for prospective Latter-Day Saints missionaries, issued in 1889, assumed that the men would "become quite attached to each other."[33]

Perhaps even more striking, given current Mormon intolerance of same-sex sexuality, were the published descriptions of the relationships of two prominent nineteenth-century Mormons. Evan Stephens, director of the famous Mormon Tabernacle Choir from 1890 to 1916, formed a series of intense attachments with "dear boy chums." At sixteen, Stephens left his parents' home and moved in with his "dearest friend" John Ward. When Ward married after about six years, Stephens lived with a succession of what the Mormon publication *Juvenile Instructor* termed his "numerous boys," most of whom also married but remained close to Stephens. *Children's Friend*, another Mormon publication, described the "last of his several life companions, who have shared his home life." Tom S. Thomas Jr. was eighteen when he went to live with the fifty-seven-year-old Stephens. After putting through college his "blond Viking who captured the eye of everyone as a superb specimen of manhood," Stephens left his position with the Tabernacle Choir to move to New York, where Thomas entered medical school. They lived together in Greenwich Village, which by then was the site of a nascent gay and lesbian community.[34]

The same issue of *Children's Friend* that carried the story of Stephens's life and loves also paid tribute to the relationship of Louie B. Felt, president of the Mormon organization for young children, and May Anderson, who worked in Felt's organization and edited *Children's Friend*. Felt's intimacies with women began within her polygynous marriage when she "fell in love" with a woman named Lizzie Mineer and asked her husband to marry her. But it was Anderson who came to share Felt's life. "Those who watched their devotion to each other declare that there never were more ardent lovers than these two." They moved in together, and Felt's husband went to live with his other wives. "Unless duty called them away from each other," they never separated. "When they were too tired to sit up any longer they put on their bathrobes and crawled into bed to work until the wee hours of the night."[35] The story of Felt and Anderson, like that of Evan Stephens, suggests that gender-segregated organizations and institutions within Mormon culture fostered the same kinds of same-sex ties that we find in other single-sex environments.

Turning to a very different world, prostitution cultivated same-sex communities of women who lived together and sometimes formed close and loving bonds. Scraps of evidence suggest that at least some frontier prostitutes had sex with each other. A story circulated in the Comstock lode in northwestern Nevada, for example, that the infamous Calamity Jane had been ejected from a brothel for corrupting the inmates. In another incident in the area, a male audience at a show discovered that a flirtatious gentleman was really a woman.[36] In San Francisco in the 1870s, a woman named Jeanne Bonnet, who dressed as a man, visited the local brothels and won prostitutes away from their pimps. Bonnet had sworn to "step in between as many women" and the men who lived off them as possible. As a result, Bonnet met a violent death at the hands of an angry man, shot through the window while preparing to get into bed with a woman named Blanche Buneau.[37]

The connection between prostitutes and same-sex activity was hardly unique to the West.[38] As early as the 1840s, a pioneering study of Paris prostitutes found that a large percentage engaged in sexual acts with other women. The author concluded, perhaps not unreasonably, that "repugnance for the most disgusting and perverse acts . . . which men perform on prostitutes" drove what he called "these unfortunate creatures to lesbian love."[39] Richard von Krafft-Ebing, the German sexologist who would introduce the term "homosexual," agreed. "Disgusted with the intercourse with perversive and impotent men," prostitutes "seek compensation in the sympathetic embrace of persons of their own sex."[40] At bottom, prostitutes seemed too sexual to be women, so it was not surprising that they, like men, might lust after women.

Our images of the western frontier are rife with rowdy whores with hearts of gold carousing with drunken miners and cowboys. Ironically, such encounters highlight the mixed-gender interactions of people who lived in separate and predominantly single-sex communities. In such environments same-sex affection, love, and desire have left only traces, although they may well have flourished.

Transgressing the Boundaries of Gender

Segregated communities of women and men on the frontier promoted not only same-sex love and sexuality, but also transgressions across the boundary of gender. We have already seen two women who dressed as men hanging out at brothels. The notorious Jeanne Bonnet, born in Paris in 1849, by the time he was fifteen "cursed the day she was born a female instead of a male," according to local newspaper accounts. Described as a "man-hater" with "short cropped hair, an unwomanly voice, and a masculine face which harmonized excellently with her customary suit of boys' clothes, including a jaunty hat which she wore with all the grace of an experienced hoodlum," he faced constant arrest for wearing male attire. Undaunted, he proclaimed that the police "might arrest me as often as they wish—I will never discard male attire as long as I live."[41] And in fact he died having just smoked his pipe, drunk a glass

Front cover of the New Orleans *Mascot*, October 21, 1893, showing
the association between prostitution and lesbianism. Courtesy of
Special Collections, Tulane University Library, New Orleans.

of cognac, and removed his male clothing to climb into bed with Blanche.[42]

San Francisco, in the aftermath of the Gold Rush, sheltered several other passing women whose existence has come to light. A wealthy woman, Lillie Hitchcock Coit, dressed in men's clothes to haunt nightspots, Charlie Parkhurst drove a Wells Fargo stagecoach and even voted, and another "freak of fancy," according to a newspaper account, earned denunciation for "deceiving the opposite sex."[43] As in early modern Europe, women in the American West dressed in male clothing for a variety of reasons, but their transgression across the line of gender always held the potential of same-sex sexuality.

For men, wearing female clothes had a different set of meanings, gaining them no privileges of mobility or occupation. Yet some men did don dresses, sometimes regularly and more often in jest. In the 1860s and 1870s, a company laundress attached to Custer's Seventh Cavalry married a succession of soldiers. In 1878 this "Mrs. Nash" was living with a corporal at Fort Meade in the Dakota Territory when she died suddenly while the corporal was away from the garrison. Only when the women went to lay her out did they discover that the always heavily veiled woman was really a man. In response to his comrades' ridicule, Mrs. Nash's husband killed himself.[44]

In the other cases of cross-dressed white men, the implications for same-sex sexuality are much less clear. Cowboys at dances with few women sometimes marked their "female" cowboy partners by tying a scarf on their arms. Edgar Beecher Bronson, in his 1908 *Reminiscences of a Ranchman,* described a tall blonde in drag dancing with another cowboy. Dancing the first set "made 'Miss De Puyster' the belle of the day and night."[45]

Cross-dressing among the white inhabitants of the frontier must be considered in light of cross-gender Native Americans, who had raised such alarm among the first European immigrants. Cross-gender individuals of both biological sexes could be found in many of the Native American societies living on the frontier of white settlement, and their existence did not go unremarked. A Kutenai "female berdache," described by one commentator as "the Woman that carried a Bow and Arrows and had a Wife," appeared at Fort Astoria in Oregon in 1811.[46] George Devereux, a Freudian psychiatrist, reported the story of Sahaykwisa, a Mohave woman who married three women in succession. Devereux labeled Sahaykwisa, known as a *hwame* by the Mohaves, "a Lesbian transvestite" in his 1937 study. According to informants, men teased the wives, saying, "Why do you want a *hwame* for a husband? A *hwame* has no penis; she only pokes you with her finger." Although at the beginning the first wife replied, "That is all right for me, if I wish to remain with her," eventually all the wives deserted Sahaykwisa because of the ridicule.[47]

Far more common were reports of cross-dressed men. Those who encountered them in the West echoed the disgust of the first Spanish, French, and English invaders. "Sodomy is a crime not uncommonly committed," wrote Edwin James in *Account of an Expedition from Pittsburgh to the Rocky Mountains in the Years 1819 and '20*.[48] About the Chippewa people, Thomas A. McKenney noted in 1826, "Nothing can induce these men-women to put off these imitative garbs, and assume again the pursuits and manly exercises of the chiefs."[49] And anthropologist Matilda Coxe Stevenson, who did fieldwork among the Zunis in 1896–97, noted circumspectly that "there is a side to the lives of these men which must remain untold. They never marry women, and it is understood that they seldom have any relations with them." When We'wha, one of these Zuni "men-women," or *ihamana* in Zuni, visited Stevenson in Washington, all who met We'wha assumed she/he was a biological woman.[50]

We'wha (d. 1896) wearing the ceremonial regalia of Zuni women.
Neg. no. 85-8666. Courtesy of the National Anthropological
Archives, Smithsonian Institution, Washington, D.C.

But there are also some tantalizing suggestions of interactions between cross-gender Native American men and white men on the frontier. Peter Grant, who lived among the Sauteux Chippewas early in the nineteenth century, knew several berdaches. In his memoir of life among the Chippewas in the 1820s, John Tanner told of a fifty-year-old Chippewa, Ozaw-wen-dib, who had had many husbands and made it clear that she wanted to live with Tanner. "She often offered herself to me, but not being discouraged with one refusal, she repeated her disgusting advances until I was almost driven from the lodge." Nevertheless, Tanner was not too disgusted to accompany Ozaw-wen-dib several days later on a journey to another lodge, where he found relief when the host added her to his household of two wives. "This introduction of a new intimate into the family . . . occasioned some laughter and produced some ludicrous incidents, but was attended with less uneasiness and quarreling than would have been the bringing in of a new wife of the female sex," Tanner noted.[51]

Another intriguing account comes from a cowboy's 1903 reminiscences about the 1880s. He described how a group of cowboys "became occupied by a controversy over the sex of a young Indian—a Blackfoot—riding a cream-colored pony . . . distinguished by beads and beaver fur trimmings in the hair." He thought the young Indian was female, but one of his buddies disagreed, and to find out "rode alongside the young Indian, pretending to admire the long plaits of hair, toyed with the beads, pinched and patted the young Blackfoot." Asked if she wanted to be his "squaw," the Blackfoot smiled and replied, "Me buck."[52]

Whatever such incidents mean, it seems likely that crossdressing and traversing the gender line were more common in the West than elsewhere in American society. We can only speculate on what impact the phenomenon of the berdache had on white women and men who changed their gender, but perhaps the fact that Native American societies throughout much of the frontier region made a conceptual place for "third gender" people made a difference. In any case, the persistence of a cross-gender role among Native Americans shows that the dominant European American sexual system is not the only one we need to comprehend in order to understand sexuality in the United States.

As white settlers continued to encroach on Indian lands, the United States government tightened its grip through large-scale programs of land expropriation, confinement to reservations, and forced assimilation. Sexuality represented a key area in which Indians, the missionaries and government agents believed, needed to be taught to behave properly. That meant toning down any sexual expressiveness and, of course, toeing the gender line. In the 1870s the government agent assigned to the Hidatsas forced a berdache to cut her hair and wear men's clothing, prompting her flight to the Crow reservation. There too a government agent tried to make what the Crows called *badés* conform to white ideas of proper gender roles. An anthropologist, in 1907, described Osh-Tisch, a Crow *badé:* "Dressed as a woman, he might have passed for one except for his affectedly piping voice. Agents, I learnt, had repeatedly tried to make him put on masculine clothing, but the other Crow protested, saying it was against his nature."[53] A Baptist missionary on the reservation also denounced Osh-Tisch, warning other men to stay away. Such sanctions could not be resisted in the boarding schools that separated Indian children from their communities. A Navajo woman remembers that her cousin, what the Navajos called a *nadle,* was sent to the girls' school in Carlisle because of her dress. During a lice infestation, the authorities, to their horror, discovered her biological sex and sent her away, to what fate the Navajo woman never knew.[54] Religious and government authorities continued to do their best to wipe out gender crossing in Native American cultures, although they never entirely succeeded.

"Gentle Boys" from the "Dangerous Classes"

Back East, on the other side of the metaphorical tracks, a different kind of sex-segregated culture began to emerge by the mid-nineteenth century. At this point American cities, like European urban centers in earlier centuries, began to provide the numbers, mobility, and anonymity that made same-sex sexual subcultures viable. With the emergence of an urban working class came the formation of a culture in which sexuality was more public and, for women, less confined to marriage than was thought to be characteristic of the middle class. Until late in the century this working-class subculture was overwhelmingly heterosexual for women, but men began earlier to make contact with other men for both intra- and interclass sexual encounters.

We can find glimpses into this world through an unlikely window: the "rags to riches" novels of American hero Horatio Alger Jr. Dismissed in 1866 from his Unitarian ministry in Brewster, Massachusetts, for what the church committee of inquiry baldly called "the abominable and revolting crime of unnatural familiarity with *boys*," Alger moved to New York to begin anew.[55] He took up not only writing his famous stories but also the work of "rescuing" working-class boys from the streets. In common with other writers and reformers not known for overt sexual interest in boys, Alger glorified the affection and support of older, powerful men for "gentle" boys from the "dangerous classes." What first interested the men in particular boys was their looks. In *Ragged Dick*, Alger wrote, "In spite of his dirt and rags there was something about Dick that was attractive. It was easy to see if he had been clean and well dressed he would have been decidedly good looking." In *Phil the Fiddler*, "In spite of the dirt, his face was strikingly handsome." In *Jed the Poorhouse Boy*, "He was a strongly-made and well-knit boy of nearly sixteen, but he was poorly dressed . . . . Yet his face was attractive."[56] Taken by the contrast between a handsome if dirty face and a rag-clad body, older men began the process of "seducing" boys away from street life and the temptation to fall into a life of crime. Like Henry Higgins with Eliza Doolittle, elite men in Alger's stories saw the potential in their subjects; like other real-life elite men drawn to working-class women as the embodiment of sexual expressiveness, men like Horatio Alger found cross-class interactions erotically charged.

Within the "dangerous classes," all-male worlds fostered a concept of masculinity that contrasted with the middle-class ideal of domesticity, with its emphasis on male responsibility and self-control. If working-class men had lost their economic independence and could not achieve manliness in the workplace, they could still be tough and strong. The "manly art" of prizefighting expressed these working-class values and fostered a homoerotic aesthetic. In an environment of male camaraderie, boxers slugged it out, admired as much for their beauty as for their pugilistic skill. As one sporting journal described a boxer, "His swelling breast curved out like a cuirass: his shoulders were deep, with a bold curved blade, and the muscular development of the arm large and finely brought out."[57]

The homoeroticism of male working-class culture attracted upper- and middle-class men interested in same-sex encounters. The poet Walt Whitman sought out working-class men in the streets of Manhattan, Brooklyn, and Washington, D.C. A story he published in 1841, as a young teacher on Long Island, described the interest of working-class men in a thirteen-year-old boy. A group of sailors in an inn grab the boy. " 'There, my lads,' " says one, " 'There's a new recruit for you. Not so coarse a one, either,' he added as he took a fair view of the boy, who, though not what is called pretty, was fresh and manly looking, and large for his age." Whitman's alter ego in the story, a twenty-year-old, in Horatio Alger fashion saves the lad and offers to share his bed in the inn. "As they retired to sleep, very pleasant thoughts filled the mind of the young man . . . . All his imaginings seemed to be interwoven with the youth who lay by his side; he folded his arms around him, and, while he slept, the boy's cheek rested on his bosom."[58]

If this smacks of male romantic friendship, suggesting the difficulty of separating eroticism from that relationship, other of Whitman's writings show that he frequented taverns, parks, public baths, and other places where he encountered working-class boys. His *Daybooks* provide lists of boys he met: "Hugh Harrop boy 17 fresh Irish wool sorter . . . Robt Wolf, boy of 10 or 12 rough at the ferry . . . little black-eyed Post boy at ferry, Paddy Connelly . . . Harry Caulfield, 19, printer," and so on.[59] Whitman's diaries record his practice of taking men home for the night: "Jerry Taylor, (NJ.) of 2d dist. reg't slept with me last night . . . Saturday night Mike Ellis—wandering at the cor of Lexington av. & 32d st.—took him home to 150 37th street."[60]

In the late 1850s Whitman lived for a time in New York in his family home with Fred Vaughan, the boy who seemingly inspired him to write his homoerotic "Calamus" poems, in which he celebrated male comradeship:

> I will therefore let flame from me the burning fires that were
>   threatening to consume me,
> I will lift what has too long kept down those smouldering
>   fires,
> I will give them complete abandonment,
> I will write the evangel-poem of comrades and of love,

(For who but I should understand love, with all its sorrow
  and joy?
And who but I should be the poet of comrades?)

And:

It shall be customary in all directions, in the houses and
  streets, to see manly affection,
The departing brother or friend shall salute the remaining
  brother or friend with a kiss.[61]

Fred Vaughan married, like so many of the boys who later
passed through Whitman's life, and Whitman moved on to
Washington, where he served as a nurse to Union soldiers
wounded in the course of the Civil War. As he wrote to his
mother in 1863, "I believe no men ever loved each other as
I & some of these poor wounded, sick & dying men love
each other." To a friend, he described "how one gets to love
them, often, particular cases, so suffering, so good, so manly &
affectionate . . . lots of them have grown to expect as I leave
at night that we should kiss each other, sometimes quite a
number, I have to go round—poor boys, there is little petting
in a soldier's life in the field."[62] It was in Washington that
Whitman met Peter Doyle, to whom he remained attached
for almost a decade. The teenage Doyle met the nearly fifty-
year-old Whitman on a streetcar. Later Doyle described the
scene: "We felt to each other at once . . . . something in him
drew me that way . . . . We were familiar at once—I put my
hand on his knee—we understood."[63] Whitman recorded
his agonizing struggle to control his feelings for Doyle in
his diary, swearing "TO GIVE UP ABSOLUTELY & *for good,
from the present hour, this* FEVERISH, FLUCTUATING, *useless,*
UNDIGNIFIED PURSUIT."[64] Doyle, like Fred Vaughan before
him, was succeeded in Whitman's affections by a series of
men, all younger and working-class.

Walt Whitman and Peter Doyle, 1865. Courtesy of
the Library of Congress Photograph Collection.

The city streets in which Alger and Whitman found male companionship were less sex segregated than the other communities we have explored here, yet they were still primarily a male domain. That urban world points the way to what would later in the century become a central site for the emergence of a recognizable same-sex subculture. By 1889 G. Frank Lydston, a Chicago doctor, would make the startling assertion, "There is in every community of any size a colony of male sexual perverts; they are usually known to each other, and are likely to congregate together."[65]

East and West, worlds of women and worlds of men formed in the course of the nineteenth century, promoting same-sex interactions of very different kinds. But the sex-segregated worlds of cowboys and miners, Mormon missionaries and leaders, prostitutes and romantic friends, were no lasting fixture on the American scene. At the turn of the nineteenth century, the separate spheres of women and men began to break down, triggering another transformation of the sexual system with important consequences for the history of same-sex love and sexuality.

Four

In 1993, on the heels of Colorado's Amendment 2, which prohibited local governments in the state from outlawing discrimination against gay men, lesbians, or bisexuals, the city of Cincinnati passed a version of the legislation known as Issue 3. Issue 3 forbade Cincinnati from enacting or enforcing civil rights protections based on sexual orientation. The lawyers fighting against Issue 3 wanted to put together a homegrown case, and their search for potential expert witnesses led them to Columbus and to me and my sociologist partner, Verta, among others. When I met with the lawyers heading up the case, I found that we spoke different languages. What they—especially an attorney from the American Civil Liberties Union—wanted to hear was that history shows that people are born gay, have been discriminated against in the same ways African Americans and other people of color have suffered, and thus deserve the same kinds of legal protections. Trying to explain my view of the history of same-sex sexuality made me sweat. When I mentioned that some scholars consider race as well as sexuality socially constructed—after all, what it means to be "black" is not the same in Brazil, say, as in the United States—they seemed to think I had taken leave of my senses.

But the last straw was the concept of "political lesbians." They had heard that some women identify as lesbians even though they are not in sexual relationships with other women, but I don't think they really believed it. When I told them, in response to their questions, that an article that Verta and I had written together used the term "political lesbians" and discussed the fluid identity of such women, they immediately, and I imagine with a sigh of relief, scratched us off the list. This was not a concept they wanted mentioned in court! How could the law protect a category with so little stability?

It was a sobering experience for me. I felt frustrated that I could not explain my understanding of the history of same-sex sexuality in a way that made sense to them, and I felt useless in the important legal struggles for our community. How could the scholarly explanations that many of us have striven to construct be so dangerous? Did we really have to violate our scholarship and argue that people are simply born gay and always have been? Because the meanings of same-sex sexuality have differed across time and place and among different groups of the population in the same time and place, should discrimination be allowed?

Since this experience I have taken courage from Lisa Duggan's brilliant and creative argument that we should take as our model religious toleration, rather than civil rights based on race and gender.[1] That is, sexual desire, like religion, is not biological or fixed, but neither is it trivial or glibly changed. Sexual difference can be seen as a form of dissent. Religious liberty and religious dissent are principles the American public—and perhaps especially the forces of the religious right arrayed against those whose sexuality differs from the heterosexual—holds dear. It is an intriguing approach that I think has a great deal to commend it.

The ongoing debate over the societal consequences of different understandings of sexuality takes us back to the end of the nineteenth century, when "homosexuality" and "heterosexuality" first came into being as categories into which people might be placed and might place themselves. As we have seen, expressing desire for a person of the same sex, or engaging in a same-sex sexual act, or falling in love with someone of the same sex did not traditionally mean that one merited designation as a special kind of person. All that began to change with the creation of the categories "homosexual" and "heterosexual." In this chapter we consider the sexual transformations that swept across American society in the decades on either side of 1900. With the rise of a consumer society came increased emphasis on sexual expressiveness and public discussion of sexuality. Subcultures of those with same-sex desires began to coalesce, developing further what we have already glimpsed through the experiences of Horatio Alger and Walt Whitman. Doctors known as "sexologists"—dedicated to unraveling the mysteries of human sexuality and treating sexual dysfunction—began to articulate the problem of what they called "homosexuality" and sex "inversion." But they did not make up these concepts out of thin air. The expanding subcultures provided the inspiration for their ideas, suggesting that the doctors' definitions and the identities of men and women engaged in same-sex sexual activities interacted in a complex fashion. Walt Whitman moved in an urban male subculture that the experts would have labeled "inverted," but this was not a term he applied to himself. The newly articulated sexual categories had particular impact on romantic friends. Now more likely to be viewed with suspicion, they sometimes maintained their relationships untouched by the swirl of new ideas, sometimes reacted defensively, and sometimes embraced the labels of the medical profession, suggesting a far from simple relation between behavior and ideology. Furthermore, the new ideas about same-sex sexuality by no means entirely displaced older conceptions, as we can see by looking at men who had sex with other men in early twentieth-century Long Beach, California, and Newport, Rhode Island.

The Sexual Revolution

The sexual revolution of the turn of the century—or what has also been called the rise of sexual liberalism—meant greater public acceptance of sexual expressiveness. As the existence of prostitution and sexual subcultures in the nineteenth century makes clear, the sexualization of society that we associate with the sexual revolution was a matter of degree. Most striking was the growing public acceptance of "respectable" white women's sexuality, the spread of sexual expressiveness from the urban working class to the middle class, and increasing public discussion and expression of sexuality. The shift to a consumer society, accompanied by the growth of the advertising industry, and the continuing process of urbanization underlay the changes in sexual attitudes and behavior.

The bubbling up of the sexual underworld that brought about what looked like the sexualization of society prompted the breakdown of public barriers between women and men: young women and men had more freedom to participate in heterosocial leisure pursuits and to form heterosexual relationships outside courtship and marriage. The sexual revolution had mixed consequences for same-sex sexuality. On the one hand, the relentless "heterosexualization" of society limited opportunities for same-sex interaction and raised the specter of sexuality in every interaction between individuals of the same sex. On the other hand, newly formulated ideas about same-sex sexuality helped to publicize an identity that individuals might embrace, inadvertently contributing to the growth of what would become gay and lesbian subcultures.

"Colonies of Male Sexual Perverts"

The Chicago doctor who reported on the colonies "of male sexual perverts" lurking in every city of any size was typical of the observers whose interest in same-sex subcultures produced a written, if disapproving, record for posterity. A sex manual for males, written by Dr. George Napheys in 1871, referred to an urban sexual underworld, including "restaurants frequented by men in women's attire, yielding themselves in indescribable lewdness," in which men could meet each other for sexual encounters.[2] Psychiatrist G. Alder Blumer of the Utica Asylum in New York State reported in 1882 that one of his patients told him of being "on several occasions . . . approached by men of unnatural desire"; he also asserted that such individuals "are able to recognize each other."[3] A Saint Louis doctor, C. H. Hughes, in 1893 described what he called "an Organization of Colored Erotopaths" in Washington, D.C. According to his account, cooks, barbers, waiters, and "some even higher in the social scale" decked themselves out in "low-necked dresses . . . feathered and ribboned headdresses, garters, frills, flowers, ruffles, etc. and deport themselves as women." A queen, naked but for a ribbon on his penis, "is subject to the gaze and osculations in turn, of all the members of this lecherous gang of sexual perverts and phallic fornicators."[4] Yet what troubled observers even more than the sight of "colored erotopaths" was interracial same-sex activity, in which, they thought, race substituted for sex difference, African American men taking the "female" role. One doctor, having attended a mixed-race dance, described the men as "homosexual complexion perverts."[5]

Such subcultures were a part of the underworld of commercialized sex and vice—remember the association between prostitution and female same-sex sexuality—that grew up in the poor sections of cities. For the most part, such subcultures catered to men and not to women, who had less freedom of movement given their domestic responsibilities and the violence of the city streets. But it is clear that previously isolated women were beginning to find each other in public. Charles Nesbitt, yet another doctor, testified that in the 1880s and 1890s "perverts of both sexes maintained a sort of social set-up in New York City, had their places of meeting, and advantage of the police protection for which they could pay." He described beer gardens, dance halls, and city streets in New York and Philadelphia where effeminate men and masculine women congregated. In New York Dr. Nesbitt met a "big, not especially good-looking, red-headed girl" who worked as a detective for the city. "She was quite plainly and as mannishly dressed as the styles of that time would permit. . . . Her sort occupied a relatively higher social plane than the male prototypes," according to Nesbitt. "Not many of them commercialized their peculiarities as such. They were usually occupied in some gainful way otherwise, while many of them were married and lived in homes of their own, to all outward appearances with perfect respectability."[6]

Dr. Nesbitt seemed more comfortable with the "masculine females" than what he called "queer creatures," "fairies," and "perverts" whose attention he seemed to attract. His observation that the women did not often "commercialize their peculiarities" suggests that not until the early decades of the twentieth century did a female public world of same-sex sexuality emerge on anything close to the scale of the male subculture.

The emergence of urban subcultures of men and women who acted on their desires for same-sex sexual encounters paved the way for the development of the concept of a homosexual identity. The doctors who wandered the streets of American cities and wrote reports on what they saw carried from the urban subcultures ideas about what made the kind of people they watched tick.

Defining Inversion

From the mid-nineteenth century on, the medical profession had begun to distinguish among different kinds of nonprocreative sexuality, and this process led to defining same-sex sexuality as a particular kind of perversion. At first the medical literature conceptualized the desire for sexual relations with a member of one's own sex as a symptom—not the defining characteristic—of what was called "inversion." Inversion meant thinking, acting, and feeling in total violation of one's expected gender. According to sexologist George Beard, writing in 1884, "Men become women and women men, in their tastes, conduct, character, feelings and behavior."[7] Naturally passive women and sexually aggressive men traded natures. In an early description of a "Case of Sexual Perversion," P. M. Wise told of a woman institutionalized for passing as a man. She "embraced the female attendant in a lewd manner and came near overpowering her . . . . Her conduct on the ward was characterized by the same lascivious conduct, and she made efforts at various times to have sexual intercourse with her associates."[8] In other words, she acted like an out-of-control man. James G. Kiernan, writing in a Chicago medical journal in 1892, introduced the term "homosexual" to the

United States audience, but he meant persons whose "general mental state is that of the opposite sex."[9] Kiernan took the concept from the Viennese psychiatrist Richard von Krafft-Ebing's monumental work *Psychopathia Sexualis,* published in German in 1886. Krafft-Ebing stirred together physical traits, cross-gender behavior, and sexual desire in whipping up the category "lesbian." He discerned four types of lesbians: "normal"-appearing women who responded to the approach of masculine women; women who preferred male clothing; "inverts" who assumed "a definitely masculine role"; and full-blown homosexuals, who possessed "of the feminine qualities only the genital organs; thought, sentiment, action, even external appearance are those of a man."[10] Likewise, those who described male inverts zeroed in on gender transgression. Doctors noted that one man "never smoked and never married; [and] was entirely averse to outdoor games" and that another enjoyed "looking in the mirror . . . [and] talk[ed] in a squeaking, effeminate voice."[11]

Within a few decades, sexologists began to move away from the idea of gender transformation and to focus more specifically on same-sex sexual object choice as the defining characteristic of a new category of "homosexuals." That is, desire for sexual intimacy with an individual of one's own sex increasingly came to be seen by the good doctors less as a natural corollary of gender inversion and more as the central problem. In 1913 British sexologist Havelock Ellis defined sexual inversion as referring to sexual impulses "turned toward individuals of the same sex, while all the other impulses and tastes may remain those of the sex to which the person by anatomical configuration belongs."[12] In the case of men, Sigmund Freud detached gender nonconformity from same-sex sexual desire altogether, changing the meaning of the word "inversion" to what would come more frequently to be called "homosexuality." "The most complete mental masculinity can be combined with [male] inversion," Freud wrote.[13] Yet it was harder for the sexologists to conceive of women who sought other women as their lovers as anything other than masculine, leading to rampant confusion about the "feminine" women who desired other women.

In line with the trend in late nineteenth-century medicine, the doctors and psychologists eagerly looked for physical causes for same-sex desire. This produced a kind of paternalistic liberalism that criticized harsh legal sanctions and religious condemnation directed at "the homosexual." If people were born "inverted" or "perverted," how could society reject them for what they could not help? In place of denunciation, the doctors offered pity and pathology. G. Frank Lydston, in 1889, criticized the tendency to view "the unfortunate class of individuals who are characterized by perverted sexuality" as having "moral responsibility" for their behavior when they should, he insisted, be treated as "victims of a physical and incidentally of a mental defect."[14] Some argued that those acting on same-sex desire could only be hermaphrodites, statistical oddities combining features of both sexes. A number of sexologists who themselves sought out same-sex relations, including the German Karl Ulrichs and Magnus Hirschfeld and the British Edward Carpenter, seized the biological notion of hermaphroditism but transformed it into a mind/body split, conceptualizing a female spirit trapped in a male body or vice versa. The claim of representing a third or "intermediate" sex held powerful appeal, for despite assumptions that such people were defective, the logical conclusion was that they should not be punished.

The emphasis on biology—and the lingering diagnosis of hermaphroditism—also carried assumptions about the bodies of "inverts." In particular, the persistent fancy in Western culture that women who had sex with other women had to have an enlarged clitoris ("one vagina plus one vagina equals

The sexologists
define inversion:
photographs of a
cross-dressing man
in Austin Flint,
"A Case of Sexual
Inversion, Probably
with Complete Sexual
Anaesthesia," *New
York Medical Journal,*
December 2, 1911.

zero," as a classic sex manual of the 1970s put it) surfaces in the work of the sexologists.[15] And here racial stereotypes came into play, the female equivalent of the myth of the well-endowed black man. A study sponsored by the Committee for the Study of Sex Variants in New York in the 1930s shows how these ideas persisted, not just in popular culture but in the medical profession as well. But not only did the doctors identify elongated clitorises among African American subjects, some of the women themselves claimed with enthusiasm that their physiology allowed them to please their lovers better than a man could. Myrtle, an African American vaudevillian, reported that her clitoris grew when she "started going with women . . . . I insert my clitoris in the vagina just like the penis of a man . . . . Women enjoy it so much they leave their husbands." Another black woman, Susan, also bragged about her prowess: "I think they are fond of me because of my

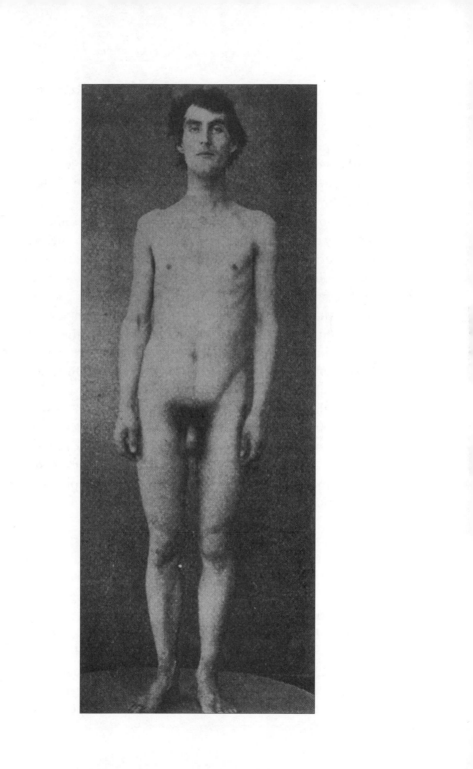

large clitoris. I think that's the chief reason. They comment upon it. They whisper among themselves. They say, 'She has the largest clitoris.' "[16] In women's embrace of the medical stereotypes (and possibly their leg-pulling of the experts) we see the elaborate process of interaction between "subject" and doctor, between interpretations within a same-sex subculture and definitions imposed from without.

Although some experts had argued early on that same-sex sexuality could be acquired, especially by those who engaged in masturbation, the spread of Freudian theory gave an enormous boost to the idea that social factors were at work in producing same-sex desire. Freud looked to developments within the family to explain the deviant state of homosexuality, thus taking same-sex sexual desire out of the realm of the biological. Yet other experts continued to cling to at least partially physiological explanations. C. P. Oberndorf separated individuals engaging in same-sex sexuality based on the way they participated in sexual acts. In his eyes, "passive" lesbians and "aggressive" homosexual men—in other words, those who behaved "appropriately" but just had sex with the wrong-sex person—resulted from social factors. But "biological anomalies of development which are often coupled with unmistakable physical signs" had to be called up to explain masculine women and feminine men.[17]

Over the years, then, the doctors who witnessed the emergence of urban subcultures that fostered same-sex sexuality struggled to come to grips with this particular kind of sexual deviance. That they shifted from definitions focusing on gender violations to ones highlighting the sex of desired partners, and that they offered social as well as biological explanations, does not mean any of these questions were settled, then or now. But their discussions do remind us that contemporary debates over these issues have a long history. Perhaps most important, by the early twentieth century the "experts" had accepted the notion that same-sex sexual desire might serve as the defining characteristic of individuals.

"I'm Not an Invert," Says Walt Whitman

That the experts debated how to define persons inclined to same-sex sexual desire and activity did not mean these questions were widely discussed at the end of the nineteenth century. Nor did it mean that men and women in the embryonic same-sex subcultures read the doctors' pronouncements and thought, "Aha! That's what I am!" It is impossible to know for sure what impact these emerging definitions had on people with same-sex desire or on the larger public. But we have a hint of one man's experiences through the case of Walt Whitman.

As we have seen, Whitman's surviving private writings attest to his interest in men, and his poems celebrate male friendship and sexuality. But he never admitted a sexual interest in men, and he even explicitly denied that his poetry dealt with male same-sex sexuality. In 1890 the British writer John Addington Symonds, familiar with the new definitions of "sexual inversion," asked Whitman directly if his concept of "comradeship" involved "those semi-sexual emotions & actions which no doubt occur between men?" Whitman responded with a denial and a denunciation of such "morbid inferences."[18] Was he simply lying (as he no doubt was when he boasted to Symonds that he had fathered six children)? Or did he speak such a different language that his take on love between men had nothing to do with the nascent notion of inversion and "homosexuality"?

There is some evidence that Whitman may have gotten into trouble with boys while teaching school on Long Island in 1841. (Remember his story about the boy and the sailors?) According to oral testimony passed down in Southold, New

York, a minister denounced him from the pulpit for "his behavior to the children," and a crowd tarred and feathered him. Whatever actually occurred, he left abruptly, his school gained the nickname "the Sodom School" because of his reputation, and for a time Whitman's literary production ground to a halt.[19]

Furthermore, Whitman used a code name and feminine pronouns when recording his misery over Peter Doyle, suggesting an uneasiness over his feelings for another man. And Whitman and his friends used the word "gay" in a way that might suggest its use by this time as a coded term for those interested in sex with men. One correspondent, in 1863, wrote of a mutual acquaintance, "I wished that I could see him this evening and go in the Ward Master's Room and have some fun for he is a gay boy."[20]

But perhaps Whitman simply did not recognize himself in the portrayals of the sexologists. In his writing he used the terms "adhesive love," "fervid comradeship," "manly friendship," and "amative love" to describe the male-centered ethic that was so important in his life. The concepts of "adhesiveness" and "amativeness" came from phrenology, the then popular science of reading one's character from the shape of the skull. Although such words mean little to us now, we cannot dismiss them as terms for Whitman's feelings while embracing only the word "gay" simply because it carries meanings we grasp more easily.

Revolutionizing Romantic Friendship

In some ways the new definitions of deviance fell most heavily on romantic friends, who could no longer always assume an innocent interpretation of their love, devotion, and physical affection. It is not that suddenly the entire world saw inverts in every same-sex couple. But the category "homosexual" opened up such a possibility, in the minds of both observers and romantic friends themselves. Psychiatric literature began in the 1910s to report homosexual activity, often interracial, among girls and women in reformatories and prisons, and while such kissing and petting and mutual masturbation might be dismissed as sexually depraved women "making do" with each other, it also raised troubling questions about what might be going on in the more respectable middle-class women's institutions such as boarding schools and colleges.[21]

We know little about what happened to the male form of romantic friendship—although I suspect that the greater visibility of male same-sex sexuality in the urban subcultures threw stronger suspicion on pairs of loving male friends—but certainly the sexual revolution cast female romantic friends in an entirely new light. In the 1870s and 1880s, women's colleges were hit by a fad known as "smashing." As an article in the Yale student newspaper described it, "When a Vassar girl takes a shine to another she straightway enters upon a regular course of bouquet sendings, interspersed with tinted notes, mysterious packages of 'Ridley's Mixed Candies,' locks of hair perhaps, and many other tender tokens, until at last the object of her attentions is captured, the two women become inseparable, and the aggressor is considered by her circle of acquaintances as—smashed."[22] But a 1928 novel about Vassar described a sea change. By 1920, "intimacy between two girls was watched with keen distrustful eyes. Among one's classmates, one looked for the bisexual type, the masculine girl searching for a feminine counterpart, and one ridiculed their devotions."[23] What had once seemed a natural, if occasionally too obsessive, relationship within the ivy-covered walls of the women's colleges now took on the taint of deviance.

Thus African American poet Angelina Weld Grimké, the grandniece of abolitionists Sarah and Angelina Grimké, in the last decade of the nineteenth century formed a romantic friendship but later obscured her love for women. As a member of the middle class, Grimké's friendship with her school friend Mamie Burrill followed the pattern common among white middle-class women. In 1896 Burrill wrote to Grimké: "Could I just come to meet thee once more, in the old sweet way, just coming at your calling, and like an angel bending o'er you breathe into your ear, 'I love you.'" Grimké, later that year, expressed her own longing: "Oh Mamie if you only knew how my heart beats when I think of you and it yearns and pants to gaze, if only for one second upon your lovely face."[24] But Grimké was always careful to veil her desires in her published poetry, pouring out the pain of a lost love only in unpublished lyrics.

Yet no wholesale rejection of romantic friendships darkened the skies. Just as only certain behaviors had triggered suspicion about female friends during the heyday of romantic friendship, so now some women went blithely about their way with no apparent concern about being mistaken for inverts or homosexuals. In the Bryn Mawr College yearbook for 1921, two graduates contributed an essay about smashing that gave absolutely no hint that the students felt any shame about the practice: "Crushes are bad and happen only to the very young and very foolish," the authors wrote with evident irony. "Once upon a time we were very young, and the bushes on the campus were hung with our bleeding hearts . . . . Only the most jaundiced mind could call by any other name than friendship Nora's tender feeling toward Gertie Steele, which led her to keep Gertie's room overflowing with flowers, fruit, candy, pictures, books, and other indispensable articles."[25]

Romantic friendships and Boston marriages lived on well into the twentieth century, even in circles exposed to the writings of the sexologists. American women active in the international women's movement moved in a world familiar with the terms "fairies," "queer," "manly-looking women,"

Angelina Weld Grimké (1880-1958). Courtesy of the Moorland-Spingarn Research Center, Howard University, Washington, D.C.

and "perverse from a sexual point of view."[26] Yet some loved and lived with women partners, with an apparent lack of self-consciousness. Consider, for instance, the relationship of Hull House founder and international peace activist Jane Addams with Mary Rozet Smith. When they traveled, they wired ahead to be sure to get a double bed.[27] When separated, Addams wrote to Smith, "I miss you dreadfully and am yours till death," and Smith expressed similar longing, writing, "You can never know what it is to me to have had you and to have you now."[28] Smith inspired a great deal of enthusiasm among Addams's colleagues. "Will you kiss your dear friend, Miss Smith, for me and tell her that in sleepless nights and even in nice dreams I see her before me as a good angel," wrote Dutch feminist Aletta Jacobs in 1915. "I have a remembrance of her as one of the sweetest women I ever met in the world," Jacobs added four years later. And, even more extravagantly, Jacobs concluded in 1923, "I always have admired her and if I would have been a man I should have fallen in love with her."[29]

Anna Howard Shaw, minister, charismatic orator, and international leader, had a reputation within suffrage circles for her "strong and passionate attachments to other women," some of which "have broken up in . . . tempestuous fashion." Shaw described her "abiding love for home and home life" at her country house, Moylan, which she shared with her partner Lucy Anthony. When Shaw fell and broke her foot and Anthony, at the same time, fractured her elbow, Shaw ruefully labeled them "rather a broken up couple." Anthony called Shaw, after her death, "my Precious Love," "the joy of my life."[30]

Or consider M. Carey Thomas, president of Bryn Mawr College and a redoubtable lady if ever there was one, who chose as her life's loves two women, with some overlap. As a student in Switzerland in the early 1880s, she formed with her Baltimore friend Mamie Gwinn what they both considered a marriage. They lived together, loved each other passionately, and left a record of kisses exchanged and heads nestled in laps.[31] By the time Thomas became president of Bryn Mawr in 1894, she was also in love with another Baltimore friend, Mary Garrett, who in addition was her financial patron. Unable to give up Gwinn's "little love" for the intense and fully requited passion of Garrett, Thomas carefully arranged the two women's comings and goings so they did not have to meet, although they of course knew of each other. But what is particularly striking about Thomas's story is the way she bridged the worlds of romantic friendship and homosexuality. For she read about lesbianism, including sexual acts between women, she admired and followed the trial of Oscar Wilde, and she kept lists of books labeled "Lesbianism" and "Books on Sapphism." While she shared a bed with the

M. Carey Thomas and Mamie Gwinn, 1879. Courtesy of the
Bryn Mawr College Archives, Bryn Mawr, Pennsylvania.

woman she loved, as had countless romantic friends, she also read texts that linked love between women and sexuality. Yet Thomas seemingly never took in any negative portrayals of lesbianism, never expressed any guilt or unease.

These women—and others like them—may have evaded a deviant label because of their class, their gender conformity, and their all-around "respectability." I doubt they ever thought of themselves as in any way "inverted." Yet some women worried that others would see them in the outlines of the new "lesbian" and as a result vehemently denied the applicability of the deviant definitions. Jeannette Marks, a Mount Holyoke professor who lived in an intimate relationship with the college president, Mary Woolley, denounced "unwise college friendships" as "abnormal" and insisted, contrary to her own life experience, that the only relationship that could "fulfill itself and be complete is that between a man and a woman."[32]

Other women may have recognized themselves somewhat uneasily in the new conceptualizations. Not as self-deluding as Marks, they fretted about whether they were homosexual and sometimes deployed the doctors' definitions to convince themselves they were not. In her 1930 autobiography, "Mary Casal" (a pseudonym) described her sexual relationship with another woman as "the very highest type of love" but insisted that "our lives were on a much higher plane than those of *the real inverts. While we did indulge in our sexual intercourse,* that was never the thought uppermost in our minds."[33] Likewise prison reformer Miriam Van Waters, who formed a deeply romantic relationship with her benefactor Geraldine Thompson, herself a married woman, struggled with the definitions. In the 1920s, when the two women first met, the concept of homosexuality was no mystery, and Van Waters had read the work of the sexologists. But "lesbianism" suggested gender inversion, the "mannish" lesbian, or a Freudian notion of pathology, and Miriam and Geraldine, like Walt Whitman, considered themselves "normal." Yet they were also careful to conceal their relationship in certain situations, and Van Waters expressed doubt about her own sexuality. When Van Waters later came under attack for tolerating homosexuality at the women's prison she supervised, she and Thompson systematically burned their letters. Van Waters did not consider her relationship with Thompson in the same category as the lesbianism among prison inmates, but she was afraid others would.[34]

In contrast to these kinds of strategies, some women embraced the new definitions as a way of claiming their own sexuality. British feminist Frances Wilder wrote in gratitude to sexologist Edward Carpenter (himself homosexual) that through reading his work she had come to realize that she "was more closely related to the intermediate sex than I had hitherto imagined."[35] Wilder's admission was unusually frank, but we can find hints in the most unlikely places that the relation between the pronouncements of the sexologists and the fashioning of identities by individual women was a dance with the most intricate footwork.

Take the tale of Alice Mitchell, a middle-class white nineteen-year-old from Memphis who in 1892 murdered the girl she loved when their plans to elope went awry.[36] At first the passion of Mitchell for Freda (known as "Fred") Ward seemed to their families to fit the mold of romantic friendship. But when Alice hatched a plot to dress as a man, marry, and support her love, the alarm bells went off. Fred's sister, with whom she lived, sent back Alice's engagement ring and other love tokens and forbade the young women to see each other. In the meantime Fred (who was traditionally feminine despite her nickname) had explored relationships with two men, much to Alice's despair. Alice then carried out an earlier threat to kill Fred if she broke her promise to marry her.

This and similar lurid tales became grist for the mill of the mass circulation newspapers and the sexologists, spreading notions of perverted female love in ever-widening circles. But within the story of Alice Mitchell we can also see two women trying to create a form for their love that went beyond romantic friendship. Alice's gender crossing evokes the "mannish lesbian" of the sexologists but also suggests that women might have clung to such a strategy as a means to act on their same-sex love and desire.

From smashing girls through Jane Addams, M. Carey Thomas, Jeannette Marks, and Miriam Van Waters to Alice Mitchell, romantic friends reacted in myriad ways to the changing world of the turn of the century. Romantic friends were not, of course, the only ones affected, as the responses of Walt Whitman and the African American "sex variant" women in the 1930s New York study make clear. All their stories, and their sometimes active engagement with new ideas about sexual deviance, allow us to see the intricacy of cause and effect in considering the relation of ideology and behavior.

The "Twentieth-Century Way"

In November 1914 police in Long Beach, California, arrested fifty men, many of them seemingly respectable, on charges of "social vagrancy." Their crimes involved deviant sexual behavior. Following up on the story, an inquisitive journalist uncovered evidence of a "society of queers" in the area of Los Angeles, reputedly numbering up to five thousand men, who gathered at private parties and "96 clubs" where they dressed in drag and participated in orgies. They also engaged in sexual acts in the public restroom of the Long Beach Bathhouse. An informer, himself part of the community, described a party at which the guests donned silk kimonos and wigs at the door, and another where the table setting included "a candy representation of a man's private which was sucked and enjoyed by each guest to the evident amusement of all."[37]

The unfortunate men who ended up in court faced charges of vagrancy rather than sodomy. According to the reporter assigned to the case, this group engaged in "nothing more nor less than 'cocksucking.' "[38] As appalling as this practice was, the investigator explained that it was not the same as "homosexualism." "It resembles homosexualism in the respect that men find their sexual pleasure and gratification with men and boys rather than women and women on the other hand are attracted sexually toward girls and women instead of the opposite sex."[39] But only anal penetration seemed to count as homosexuality. Oral sex, tellingly dubbed by the community of men who practiced it the "twentieth-century way," was perverse and deviant in its own right. But even when engaged in by men together, it was the particular sexual act, rather than the sex of the partners, that carried the most significance.

This tiny window into an early twentieth-century world suggests how important it is to recognize the shifting meanings of concepts such as "homosexuality." This becomes even clearer when we turn to the history of an investigation of same-sex sexuality at the Newport (Rhode Island) Naval Training Station just a few years later, in 1919 and 1920.[40]

The trial documents generated by the navy's investigation reveal the competing ways of viewing sexuality that coexisted in the first decades of the twentieth century. The navy, concerned about "immorality" in Newport, recruited decoys to seek out, have sex with, and testify against men who self-identified as "queers." In this they were even more ambitious than the police in Long Beach, who had hired two crusading traveling detectives to entrap men into oral sex.

According to the journalist who investigated the incident, the detectives went to the Long Beach Bathhouse and watched "until they saw a man whom they thought to be given to this sort of thing" and then attracted his attention "by putting their fingers through a hole in the board partition dividing the toilet walls. Upon looking through he would see a man's mouth close to the aperture and if [he] were that kind of man and the suspicions of the officers correct, would stick his penis through the hole."[41] At this point he would be arrested.

Officials in Newport went further still, but neither the decoys nor the other "straight" men with whom the "queers" had sexual relations were, in the navy investigators' eyes, "homosexual" in any sense of the word. This was not just a case of oral sex versus anal sex, as in Long Beach. The participation of decoys in sexual acts with other men, because they always took the so-called "masculine" or "active" role (that is, inserted their penises), had no consequences for their identity or morality. Even men who had ongoing relationships with the "queers"—known as "friends" or "husbands"—were not themselves considered queer.

The "queers" were queer because they took the receptive role in sexual acts and also adopted other feminine traits. Further, they distinguished among themselves based on what particular sexual acts they preferred. "Queers" might be "fairies," who engaged in oral sex (that twentieth-century way), "pogues," who sought out anal sex, or "two-way artists," a name that speaks for itself. An investigator indicated on one list of suspects how each could be identified in terms of such sexual tastes, but a "friend" could be identified only as someone who "went out with all the above named men at various times and had himself sucked off or screwed them through the rectum."[42] For the queers, effeminacy in appearance and sexual behavior meant a positive identity; for the navy it marked men as deviant.

The defense in this case introduced an altogether different line of interpretation by implying that any participation in a same-sex act (not simply gender inversion or taking the receptive part in a sexual act) defined an individual as deviant. By calling into question the interests of the decoys, who volunteered to have sex with the "queers," the defense suggested that all men involved in same-sex sexual relations, no matter what sexual role they played and for what purpose, shared a similar status. Listen to the following examination of a decoy:

Q. You volunteered for this work?

A. Yes, sir.

Q. You knew what kind of work it was before you volunteered, didn't you?

A. Yes, sir.

Q. You knew it involved sucking and that sort of thing, didn't you?

A. I knew that we had to deal with that, yes, sir.

Q. You knew it included sodomy and that sort of thing, didn't you?

A. Yes, sir.

Q. And you were quite willing to get into that sort of work?

A. I was willing to do it, yes, sir.

Q. And so willing that you volunteered for it, is that right?

A. Yes, sir, I volunteered for it, yes, sir.[43]

From the perspective vigorously pursued by the attorneys for the defense, effeminacy was less important than participation in a sexual act. Taking a position radically opposed to that of the navy investigators, the defense not only tried to tar the decoys with the brush of deviance but also defended a different kind of same-sex liaison. For it was not only sailors in women's clothing who found themselves dragged into court. The navy also brought charges against two middle-class professional men: an Episcopal clergyman, Samuel Kent, and a YMCA worker, Arthur Leslie Green. Although decoys testified that they had had sex with Kent, he won acquittal, and his arrest even provoked a successful protest on the part of church officials against the entire naval investigation.

What was at stake here was appropriate masculine behavior. What Kent and Green and their supporters considered "Christian brotherhood"—visiting sailors in the hospital, lending them money, showing affection and concern, opening their homes to them—could be interpreted as effeminate behavior and inappropriate interest. Witnesses described the two men as "peculiar," "sissyfied," and "effeminate," but as one put it in Kent's case, "I don't know whether you would call it abnormal. He was a minister." According to other testimony in court, Green held the hands of boys in the hospital and "talk[ed] like a woman to me," evidently a reference to the content of the conversation rather than the pitch of the voice.[44]

Newport's church officials stood solidly behind Kent and Green because lavishing attention on the boys in the navy, in the tradition of Horatio Alger, was the mark of a good minister or volunteer. Kent saw his job as "trying to be friends with them, urging them to come to my quarters and see me if they wanted to, telling them—I think, perhaps, I can best express it by saying 'Big Brotherhood.'"[45] Even Kent's invitation to a decoy to come into his bed could be explained away. The decoy had complained of being lonely and having no place to sleep, so Kent had invited him home; settled on a cot in the living room, the decoy had then said he was cold, so Kent invited him into his own bed. Pure Christian brotherhood, according to the church. Perversion, according to the navy.

The Newport investigation reveals the process of labeling in flux and shows us how little settled these issues were in the first decades of the twentieth century. Although the concept of gender inversion is evident in the self-definitions of the "queers" and in the decoys' insistence that feminine traits betrayed a "fairy," only one self-identified fairy used the medical term "invert," explaining that he had heard the term in theater circles. The medical literature played almost no part in the trial. No sexologist took the stand to analyze what was going on, and the one doctor who played a central role in the investigation did so because of his job at the naval hospital. He read up on the literature in the course of the trial but stuck to the opinion common in Newport: that there was a fundamental difference between "congenital perverts" and "normal people submitting to acts of perversion, as a great many normal people do, [who] do not become perverts themselves."[46]

This is not to suggest that the concept of inversion had no impact anywhere. At about the same time that the decoys cheerfully reported for duty, a twenty-year-old college student at Washington and Lee University in Lexington, Virginia, was falling in love with his male friends. "Jeb Alexander" (a pseudonym) wrote in his diary in 1921, "I want love and affection! Damn it! . . . I am madly in love with C. C. Dasham. 'Sexual inversion,' Havelock Ellis calls it." Alexander recognized himself in the writings of the sexologists and took courage from the identification. "This diary of mine is a tissue of posturing. My real thoughts on such matters as sex are not admitted even to myself. I *will* be frank," he wrote, just before admitting his love for Dasham.[47] Soon he graduated to cruising Lafayette Park in Washington, D.C., his hometown, though he also found the love and affection he sought in a long-term relationship with "Dash."

Likewise F. O. Matthiessen, newly graduated from Harvard and embarking on his career as a cultural historian, wrote to his lover, the painter Russell Cheney, about his reaction to reading the work of the sexologists in 1924. Having read Edward Carpenter's *The Intermediate Sex* in one day, he recalled the work of Havelock Ellis. "Then for the first time it was completely brought home to me that I was what I was by nature . . . . Was it possible for love and friendship to be blended into one?" He discovered that it was, since his relationship lasted until Cheney's death in 1945.[48]

If not representative of every tendency in the unfolding story of men's same-sex desires, the Newport investigation nevertheless throws open the curtains, affording us a full view of an early community of men engaged in same-sex sexual activity. The all-male military environment, of course, encouraged the formation of such a community by pulling young men away from their homes and enclosing them in a single-sex world. But Newport was not an utter anomaly, as was made clear by the report from Long Beach and the extensive testimony about sailors' trips to cruising grounds in other locales and visits from out-of-town men to the hot spots in Newport. In Newport, as in Long Beach, men might engage in particular sexual acts with other men and not rank as "homosexuals." If exactly what did make one queer differed from person to person and group to group, it is nevertheless clear that men with same-sex desires knew how to find others who shared their passions.

The sexual revolution had different consequences for what would come to be called heterosexuals and homosexuals. Discussion and expression of cross-sex sexuality became more public and accepted; same-sex sexuality also became more public, but it came to serve as the defining characteristic of a particular kind of deviant person. The early sexologists observed the emerging urban subcultures of men and women and tried to categorize what they saw. In turn, women and men who experienced same-sex love and desire, including romantic friends who were not part of the sexual underworld, reacted to the new definitions. Out of this tangled interaction came communities that fostered same-sex sexual identities, although these were never a mere reflection of the pronouncements from on high.

Five

COMING TOGETHER: CONTESTED

IDENTITIES AND THE EMERGENCE

OF COMMUNITIES

Sometime in the mid-1980s, Joan Nestle of the Lesbian Herstory Archives called hoping that Verta and I could help her
with an urgent matter. A woman named Marge McDonald
had died not long before in Athens, Ohio, and when her will
was read her family discovered she had left all her personal
belongings that had any significance for lesbian history to
the Archives in New York. This was the first they knew of
her lesbianism, and they were most uncomfortable about the
revelation. Their lawyer had called the Archives, and Joan was
desperate to find someone close by who could drive to Athens
and physically take charge of whatever material was there, lest
the family destroy or hide anything.

Verta and I immediately thought of two of her graduate
students, Phyllis Gorman and Kelly McCormick. We had

known them since they were undergraduates at Ohio State, before they had become a couple. Phyllis had written her master's thesis on the first lesbian homophile organization, the Daughters of Bilitis, and we knew she'd be game for this adventure. Our only concern was that Kelly (now the founder and continuing force behind the lesbian mothers' group Momazons) was at that time quite closeted, despite her relationship with Phyllis. We weren't sure how she'd feel about appearing in Athens as the embodiment of lesbianism and about dealing with a fearful family.

But go they did. The lawyer and a couple of family members gathered at the house to make sure Phyllis and Kelly didn't cart off anything inappropriate. The high point of the day came when Kelly was sorting through McDonald's record collection, putting anything lesbian or gay in one pile and all the rest in another. When she came to a Frank Sinatra record, she inadvertently put it in the gay stack. One of the family members gasped in horror. "Oh no, not him!" he exclaimed. Kelly quickly moved it to the correct pile, though she was tempted to leave it where it was.

As it turned out, Marge McDonald's diaries proved a treasure, since they recorded her first forays into the lesbian community of Columbus in the 1950s. Her chronicle evokes the still-untold story of the spread of lesbian bars and lesbian communities all across the country in the decades after the Second World War. And the tale of her bequest to the Lesbian Herstory Archives reminds us how important such stories are and how much communities are still central in the gay and lesbian worlds of the present.

In this chapter I turn to the emergence in the first half of the twentieth century of what we can begin to call lesbian and gay communities. In big cities across the nation, men and women with same-sex desires knew where to gather,

Marge McDonald, ca. 1952.
Marge McDonald Collection.
© LHEF, Inc. Courtesy of the Lesbian
Herstory Archives, Brooklyn, New York.

used certain terms to identify themselves, and developed codes of dress and behavior that marked them as particular kinds of people. But it was not just in the notorious locations that women and men were able to meet others with similar sexual desires. Communities sprang up in the most unlikely places. What is perhaps most remarkable is the variety of competing conceptions of who was "queer," to say nothing of the toleration of same-sex sexuality in certain social contexts. In the building of what came to be named "lesbian" and "gay" communities we can see the origins of the modern world we live in. But it is just as important to notice the differences.

A Different World

The time has come to talk vocabulary. By the seventeenth century the word "gay" had come to connote illicit pleasure, and by the nineteenth century it specifically referred to prostitution. Like so many other words used to describe men with same-sex desires, "gay" moved from the sexual underworld in which such desires might be fulfilled to subcultures that fostered the building of identities based on same-sex love and desire. "Gay" was in use as a code word for same-sex sexuality in the United States in the first half of the twentieth century—perhaps earlier, as Walt Whitman's correspondence suggests—but it did not come into the vocabulary of a wider public until the 1950s. The terms most in use across different ethnic groups were "queer" and "fairy" and a host of words with more precise meanings. African Americans said "faggot," "bulldagger," "ladylover," "stud," or "in the life."[1] Words changed their exact meanings over time and in the mouths of different kinds of people. What is important is that we avoid thinking that all the terms used by people in the past are synonyms for what we today mean by "gay" and "lesbian."

We must listen carefully and try to understand exactly what people were saying.

Identity as a "queer" emerged in the context of participating in a community of like-minded individuals. In cities all across the nation by the early twentieth century, a man with determination could find the place to meet the right people. In Newport, Rhode Island, the social center was the YMCA. The "gang," as they called themselves, took steps to come together beyond seeking out sex. They lived or visited at the Y, ate dinner or threw parties there. According to Edward Stevenson, who published a study titled *The Intersexes* in 1908, "Certain smart clubs are well-known for their homosexual atmospheres" in New York, Boston, Washington, Chicago, New Orleans, and Saint Louis, sometimes passing for a "literary-club," an "athletic society," a "dramatic-society," or a "chess-club," so no "outsider easily suspects what really goes on."[2]

The Vice Commission of Chicago, formed to study female prostitution, reported in 1911 on the existence there of "groups" and "colonies" of men interested in same-sex sexual activity. These men cruised the streets, gathered in particular boardinghouses, worked in certain professions, and attended theater performances that appealed to their tastes. In the 1920s and 1930s, sociologists at the University of Chicago, indulging their passion for immersing themselves in and recording urban life, left us a rich record of same-sex communities. The faculty sent students flocking to dance halls and cabarets to observe the doings of working-class city people, and there they encountered men in search of men as well as men in search of women. A true/false test in a 1938 sociology course even posed the question: "In large cities, homosexual individuals tend to congregate rather than remain separate from each other." Based on what the sociologists had observed in the streets of the city, the correct answer was "true."[3]

CHAPTER FIVE

The areas where identifiably "queer" men hung out became the places where other men interested in meeting them
knew they could go. In Chicago that area was the Near North
Side, where single men and women lived in rooming houses
and patronized restaurants, saloons, and theaters that catered
to their tastes and their limited means. Boardinghouses and
"black and tan" cabarets that attracted an interracial following
also flourished on the South Side. Private parties, news of
which spread through public gathering places, added to the
number of spots where queer men could find one another.
One man explained that he "came out . . . when I began to
go to parties." Even the workplaces, such as department stores
and offices, which attracted more than their share of gay male
employees, could function as a gay social world. One man who
had moved to Chicago knowing he would not be lonely there
"looked around the office and said to the manager, 'Why all
the fellows are sissy around here.' "[4] What one of the sociologists called the "social world of the homosexuals, where they
have their particular status, participate in common activities,
where they can express themselves in their particular fashion,"
was central to the creation of queer identities.[5]

In New York by the end of the nineteenth century, the
Bowery was home to a number of "resorts" or saloons that
catered to a flamboyant "fairy" subculture. A center of commercialized vice, the Bowery was an immigrant working-class
neighborhood where the inhabitants rubbed shoulders, on
the streets and in drinking establishments, with "boys [who]
have powder on their faces like girls and talk to you like
disorderly girls talk to men," as a middle-class investigator
reported in 1901.[6]

By the 1920s two New York neighborhoods—Greenwich
Village and Harlem—had come to be home to large and
visible same-sex enclaves. Greenwich Village, at the turn of the
century an Italian immigrant neighborhood, attracted "bo-

hemian" artists of all ethnic groups in the 1900s. What hostile observers called the "long-haired men" and "short-haired women" of the Village advocated social and sexual experimentation, creating a favorable environment for those with same-sex desires. Unconventionality, including the realm of sexual behavior, became the trademark of the Village, and in the years after the First World War its reputation drew both curious sightseers and individuals looking for tolerance. Speakeasies and tearooms catering "to the 'temperamental' element" flourished; one of these, the Flower Pot, was a "gay and impromptu place where excitement reigned from nine in the evening until the wee hours of the morning."[7] What distinguished such locales from the earlier fairy resorts of the Bowery was that straight and gay people mingled in a middle-class milieu.

But the truly "mixed" social scene, in every sense of the word, could be found in Harlem, Manhattan's major cross-class black neighborhood. There African American men and women, denied entry to establishments in other parts of the city, built a vibrant nightlife that attracted straight and gay, black and white, women and men. As an observer described one nightclub, "Every night we find the place crowded with both races, the black and the white, both types of lovers, the homo and the heterosexual."[8] The dazzling talent of the artistic flowering known as the Harlem Renaissance spread word of gay and lesbian love through such diverse channels as the literature of Claude McKay and Langston Hughes, the drawings of Bruce Nugent, and the raunchy blues lyrics of Bessie Smith. Claude McKay's 1928 novel *Home to Harlem* described a Baltimore bar where

all around the den, luxuriating under the little colored lights, the dark dandies were loving up their pansies. Feet tickling feet under tables, tantalizing liquor-rich giggling, hands busy up above.

"A Spot in the Village," illustrating the reputation of Greenwich Village in the interwar years. From *Broadway Brevities*, June 6, 1932, reproduced in George Chauncey Jr., *Gay New York*.

BORED MA

"Honey gal! Honey gal! What other sweet boy is loving you now? Don't you know your last night's daddy am waiting for you?"[9]

The blues publicized not only the existence of homosexuals but a language to describe them. Lucille Bogan's "B.D. Women Blues" sang of "bulldagger" women, and "Sissy Man Blues" gave voice to their male counterparts. Although such songs poked fun at "mannish-acting" women and "lisping, swishing, womanish-acting" men, they also served to identify and name individuals who built an identity around same-sex desire, and some of them even celebrated the gay lifestyle.[10] The terms "bulldagger"—derived from "bulldyker," referring to women "diked out" in male attire—and "sissy" called attention to the cross-gender aspects of queer life. And in fact many of the great women blues singers—Gladys Bentley,

IN THE VILLAGE   June 6, 1932

" call Percy and we'll make a party of it."

Ma Rainey, Bessie Smith, Ethel Waters, and Alberta Hunter—
were themselves lesbian or bisexual.

A variety of locations, including private and semipri-
vate parties, provided a safe place for lesbians and gay men
to meet in Harlem. The "rent party," which offered music,
dancing, and the chance to buy bootleg alcohol in return
for an admission fee, allowed the host to pay the rent and
brought together people with similar sexual interests, not
all of whom knew the host. Mabel Hampton, an African
American woman who lived in Harlem in the 1920s in her
teens, described such parties: "You buy your drinks and meet
other women and dance and have fun . . . . And most of
them was good-lookin' women too . . . the bulldykers used
to come and bring their women with them, you know. And
you wasn't supposed to jive with them, you know . . . . They

danced up a breeze."[11] Those interested in same-sex sexual encounters also attended the lavish parties thrown by A'Lelia Walker, the millionaire daughter of Madame C. J. Walker, who had made her fortune marketing her hair-straightening process. "Buffet flats," private apartments where rooms could be rented by the night and where after-hours entertainment sometimes featured live sex acts, also might cater to a gay clientele. More public were speakeasies and costume balls, which attracted a racially integrated crowd of both hetero-sexuals and homosexuals. One African American investiga-tor hired by the Committee of Fourteen, an antivice group, described the scene in a basement speakeasy in 1928. One woman "was dancing indecently with a man . . . . Several of the men were dancing among themselves. Two of the women were dancing with one another going through the motions of copulation . . . . I also observed two men who were dancing with one another kiss each other, and one sucked the other's tongue."[12]

The onset of the Great Depression brought an end to the Harlem Renaissance. Still, a gay and lesbian subculture remained, albeit one less open and less racially mixed. What is remarkable about Harlem in the 1920s is that same-sex desire and love served as a dividing line that sometimes put black and white individuals on the same side.

Women with same-sex desires had fewer options for public socializing, although by the 1920s communities be-gan to form in the furnished-room districts of Chicago and "bulldaggers" found a place in Harlem. Bisexual African American blues singer Ma Rainey immortalized State Street, on the South Side of Chicago, in such verses as

Goin' down to spread the news
State Street women wearing brogan shoes

. . . .

Mabel Hampton, 1918. © LHEF, Inc. Courtesy of
the Lesbian Herstory Archives, Brooklyn, New York.

There's one thing I don't understand
Some women walkin' State Street like a man.

"Box-Car Bertha," a female hobo who left an autobiography
for posterity, mentioned "tea shops and bootleg joints on
the near-north side" of Chicago where such women might
gather, and other commentators observed private parties and
women living together in the bohemian parts of the furnished

room district.[13] As in the dance hall subculture, women with "women sweethearts," some of whom worked as prostitutes, mixed easily in a world of commercialized and open sexuality. A sociology student saw twenty-five "queer gals," many in drag, at the Bally Hoo Café in Chicago in 1933.[14] By the late 1930s, Mona's in San Francisco had made the move from its bohemian beginnings to its new guise of a lesbian nightclub where lesbian waitresses sang show tunes and male impersonators camped it up.[15]

In all these places, and in others like them in cities across the nation, men and women met one another and built communities. As in Newport, Rhode Island, some level of gender crossing played a central role in attracting the attention of potential partners, even if the medical definitions of gender inversion did not. The Newport gang sometimes dressed in drag and adopted women's names, and even in public they might be identified as feminine. One of the naval investigators noted that "it was common knowledge that if a man was walking along the street in an effeminate manner, with his lips rouged, his face powdered, and his eyebrows pencilled," he was a "fairy." From inside the community, a member pointed to less flagrant signs: acting "sort of peculiar; walking around with his hands on his hips," a "not masculine" manner, an "expression with the eyes and the gestures."[16]

In Chicago too, effeminacy made men with same-sex desires recognizable: "In this community there is a large number of men who are thoroughly gregarious in habit; who mostly affect the carriage, mannerisms, and speech of women . . . ; who lean to the fantastic in dress and other modes of expression, and who have a definite cult with regard to sexual life . . . . They have a vocabulary and signs of recognition of their own."[17] Chicago physician William Held described a saloon in which clean-shaven male "perverts" flirted, used female names, and chatted "in a *pronounced* girl-like manner."[18]

Some Newport gang members reported effeminate tendencies from an early age, but it was the community they encountered that gave meaning to such feelings or personal styles. One man, identified by the gang not only as a "queer" but specifically as a "pogue," reported beginning to use makeup and taking a female name "because the others did" these things.[19] In Chicago, a second-generation Polish American who took part in the bohemian community learned about "queers" from novels and then heard from a friend that "fairies" hung out at the Michigan Avenue bridge. Curious, the young man hurried down to bridge, where he met a man who introduced him to his circle of friends. Seeing that they wore flashy clothes and cosmetics and acted in feminine ways, he learned to imitate them as he moved into "queer life."[20] Fairies in the Bowery dressed in women's clothing only in secure Bowery resorts or for the well-publicized drag balls that flourished in cities like New York and Chicago. But they signaled their interest in other men by dressing "as fancy and flashy as a youth" could dare, wearing such items as white kid gloves, red neckties, suede shoes, pegged trousers, or—especially bold—green suits.[21] Fairies not only wore makeup but plucked their eyebrows and lightened and waved their hair, and they "swished" when they walked.

Approaching the link between sexuality and gender from another side, one Chicago man described his attempt to alter his sexuality, to "try to be a man," by lowering his voice, walking differently, and smoking cigars after ten years of effeminacy.[22] Another dropped the fairy role from his daytime life in order to hold down "a man's job," although he took on some effeminate characteristics in the evening when he socialized with his queer friends. Although not all men who had sex with other men adopted effeminate characteristics,

"Swish," a cartoon illustrating the effeminacy of
the fairy, from *Broadway Brevities,* June 6, 1932.
Reproduced in George Chauncey Jr., *Gay New York.*

"going about with the belles," as one man put it, was what
marked one, to himself and to others, as "queer."[23]

But the existence of a community of men who expressed
their same-sex desire through effeminacy did not mean that
this world was wholly separate from the larger community.
In fact, men interested in sex with men mingled with men
seeking women in the dance halls, bars, and other hang-
outs frequented by working-class young people. In 1912 an
antivice crusader in New York observed two fairies who went
by the names Elsie and Daisy hanging out at a dance hall with a
group of women and borrowing their powder puffs.[24] Straight
men interviewed by the Chicago sociologists commented on

the presence of queers; one man expressed his dislike for men who "when they shake hands with you . . . have that peculiar look in their eyes that have a wanting feeling of expression."[25] Although some straight young men preyed on fairies, robbing, beating, or even raping them, fairies had a niche in working-class culture. An African American man described moving easily between the two worlds, having sex with both women and men. "Some of . . . [the men] you cannot tell from a woman if they never have whiskers or mustash," he added.[26] Like the "straight" men in Newport who had sex with the queers, men in the eroticized environment of the dance hall subculture might engage in sexual acts with individuals of the same or different sex.

Outside the dance halls too, men sought out sex with men without any consequences for their identity. When the fleet sailed into New York harbor, sailors might patronize female prostitutes or they might rush to the Times Square Building, known, as the owner of a newsstand there reported in 1927, as "the place to go if they want to meet fairies."[27] One Chicago man described, with a certainty that belied some anxiety, getting a blow job from a drag queen in 1933: "To myself I know in my own heart that I am not a real bitch, because a woman thrills me. A man will do when there is nothing else in the world, preferably a she man, because he is more womanly or closer to a woman."[28] If any man in the bachelor subculture of sailors, hoboes, and laborers might be tempted to have sex with another man, and to consider his masculinity enhanced by doing so, some men seemed to prefer such relationships. These men went by the names "husbands," as in Newport, "wolves," or "jockers." But even "wolves," who sought out sex with younger and slighter "punks," "lambs," or "kids," were not the same as "fairies" because they were not effeminate.[29]

In New York, the way people—both participants and observers—thought about these interactions seems to mirror

customs in the Mediterranean world from which many immigrant New Yorkers came. Italian neighborhoods sheltered "fairy resorts" far more frequently than did Jewish sections of town, and fairy folklore rated Italian men, along with Irish and African Americans, more likely than Jewish men to be interested in same-sex encounters. This may be because of the large number of single men among Italian immigrants, the traditional sex-segregation of Italian immigrant communities, and the fact that southern Italian culture in particular categorized sexual interactions according to gender and sexual role rather than the sex of the partners.[30]

In addition to housing fairies, "normal" men who had sex with them on occasion, and "wolves" who sought out such sexual contacts, big cities were also home to men who preferred sex with other men, saw themselves as different because of it, but did not express this difference through effeminacy. In New York these men identified as "queers" (note the contrast with what this label meant in Newport),

Paul Cadmus, *The Fleet's In!* 1934. Oil on canvas, NH 92806-KN. Courtesy of the Naval Historical Center, Washington, D.C.

and most were middle class. They shunned the flamboyance, effeminacy, and publicity of the fairy. As one man put it in the mid-1930s, "I don't object to being known as homosexual, but I detest the obvious, blatant, made-up boys whose public appearance and behavior provoke onerous criticism."[31] "Queer" men themselves on occasion used feminine names and adopted styles of dress and behavior that were, if not outright effeminate, certainly not traditionally masculine. But they tended to do these things in private. Jeb Alexander, the Atlanta-born man we met as he initiated his long relationship with his lover Dash, threw parties at his Washington apartment during the 1930s and 1940s. His friends sometimes wore women's clothing and engaged in what Alexander described disapprovingly as "effeminate carrying on."[32] Such disavowal of public, or all, effeminacy was very much a class difference.

We can also get a glimpse into middle-class gay worlds through the life of Richard Cowan, who graduated from

Cornell University in 1933 and went to live in Boston at the invitation of Stewart Mitchell, an editor of the literary magazine the *Dial*. Mitchell rented Cowan an apartment, and Cowan wrote in his diary that "I love S. very much," but he added that he was "incapable of being true to anyone person." He recorded his encounters with young men he met at the Symphony or the Copley Theatre or the Boston Public Garden:

Met a Dartmouth boy on the Common one night after the Symphony. His name was Jack . . . . He was a bit obvious but I liked him. He claimed he loved me etc. Stayed at his home one Saturday night while visiting some friends of his I met George, a Dartmouth boy . . . . He called me the next day & I went to the movies, with him—and that started that. I think I really did love him at first and he—very passionately—said he loved me.[33]

Clearly, middle-class men used cultural institutions such as the theater to meet comrades with similar sexual desires.

Yet the class (and age) differences between fairies and queers did not mean the creation of entirely separate social worlds. In the YMCA, residential hotels, restaurants, baths, and other public places, gay worlds developed that sometimes transcended class barriers. Middle-class queer men, like working-class fairies, sometimes sought out "normal" working-class men for sexual trysts. Charles Tomlinson Griffes, a modernist composer of the early twentieth century, had a thing for Irish policemen. In the 1910s he recorded in his diary his approaches and progress: "I talked for about 20 minutes with the policeman stationed at 42–5 in the evenings. He remembers me this time and was so responsive I asked him to go to the theater with me."[34] Men like Griffes found themselves attracted to such men's traditional masculinity, but they also found workingmen responsive to their advances.

The real class difference seemed to be between the working-class male view of sexuality and that of middle-class straight men, who had increasingly come to mark their masculinity through their sole attraction to women. No longer working with their bodies, subjected to employee status in white-collar occupations, and faced with women's demands for greater social and political power, middle-class men felt increasingly cut off from other forms of expressing virility. In this context, not only the "homosexual" but the "heterosexual" too came into being.

The visibility of same-sex sexuality and the lack of structural barriers between gay and straight worlds was most vivid in the world of entertainment. In the early 1910s, a national enthusiasm for female impersonation reached its height with the popularity of Julian Eltinge, a female impersonator with impeccable offstage masculine and heterosexual credentials. Eltinge's performances conjured up not the fairy but the gender equivalent of the minstrel in blackface: "Just as a white man makes the best stage Negro," one critic wrote, "so a man gives a more photographic interpretation of femininity than the average woman is able to give."[35] And in fact Eltinge's audiences and supporters clung to what separated him from "the usual creeping male defective who warbles soprano and decks himself in the frocks and frills of womankind." Yet despite Eltinge's emphasis on his difference from the "freaks" who "always flock together" and were " 'crazy about him,' " that they besieged him at the stage door makes it clear that they did not necessarily respect the distance he tried to maintain.[36]

By the 1920s, cross-dressing entertainers with more dubious reputations began to surface in New York. In Harlem, "Gloria Swanson," a graduate of the Chicago drag scene, and Gladys Bentley, a tuxedo-clad and top-hatted lesbian singer of impromptu raunchy lyrics, helped to make drag, if not respectable, at least a little less remarkable. Drag as entertainment led to the largest annual gathering of gay people in New York, the Hamilton Lodge Ball or Masquerade and Civic Ball, known by the late 1920s as the "Faggots' Ball." Attracting black and white spectators from across the city, the ball featured "effeminate men, sissies, wolves, 'ferries,' 'faggots,' the third sex, 'ladies of the night,' and male prostitutes . . . for a grand jamboree of dancing, love making, display, rivalry, drinking and advertisement."[37] As a "pansy craze" hit New York in the early 1930s, setting off an avalanche of entertainment featuring the kind of effeminate men that had set Eltinge's teeth on edge, the ball attracted nearly seven thousand to prance, dance, or gawk.

That respectable citizens of Harlem and other parts of New York flocked to the Faggots' Ball to take in the lavish costumes and elaborate impersonations does not, of course, mean that same-sex sexuality or gender transgression met with total approval. The antivice crusaders who went out to investigate the goings-on at queer places, as their often-hostile descriptions make clear, hoped to do away with the gay subcultures of Chicago, New York, and other cities. The authorities raided establishments known to harbor same-sex subcultures, arrested cross-dressed people or those caught in compromising positions, and censored plays, films, and novels that dealt with same-sex sexuality. The Lafayette Baths in New York suffered a police raid in 1929; a visiting German tourist reported that "various people were struck down, kicked, in short, the brutality of these officials was simply indescribable."[38] In 1920 two women wearing men's clothes were arrested in Boston. As the *Boston Post* reported the incident, the women "said they were out on a 'lark,'" but the police took them to the House of Detention, "where they were told that they would have to stay until they procured women's clothes to wear away."[39] *The Captive,* a play that opened in New York in 1926 and dealt with what the *New*

Gladys Bentley, ca. 1920s. Courtesy of the Moorland-Spingarn
Research Center, Howard University, Washington, D.C.

York Times critic called "a twisted relationship" between two women, provoked public discussion of censorship, the arrest of the producer and cast, and eventually the passage of a bill in the New York state legislature outlawing the depiction of "sex degeneracy, or sex perversion."[40] Things were far from idyllic. Still, the Faggots' Ball and pansy craze gave greater public visibility to people with same-sex desires than most people today expect to find in the past.

The Great Depression, which began in 1929, and the end of Prohibition, which had fostered a flouting of law-abiding, middle-class codes of behavior in socializing and sexuality as well as drinking, pushed the homosexual culture out of the public eye, at least in New York. Homoerotic entertainment passed out of vogue, and the mixing of gay and straight that had characterized speakeasy life came to an end. In San Francisco, in contrast, where the tourist industry touted the city's reputation for sexual license, gay men and lesbians continued to mingle with adventurous tourists who took in the drag performances at Mona's and Finocchio's.[41] The repeal of Prohibition in states (like New York) that established liquor control boards meant more, not less, government control of drinking establishments, and ironically this would give rise to the exclusively gay bar.[42] These changes set the scene for what we have come to think of as "traditional" gay and lesbian life before the late 1960s.

Urban developments in cities such as Chicago and New York do not, however, cover the whole story of identities and communities in the early twentieth century. We simply have more evidence of what went on in places where observers— often, as we have seen, hostile ones—plied their trade. In particular, they tell us little about the lives of women, providing only a glimpse of those who ventured out into the social spaces still controlled to a large extent by men. To flesh out the picture, we turn to some unlikely places far away from big-city life.

Ladies' Afternoon at the Sauna

Salt Lake City, Utah, stronghold of the Church of Latter-Day Saints, which publicly excommunicates homosexuals (despite the histories of Evan Stephens, Louie Felt, and May Anderson), sheltered an unseen lesbian community in the 1920s and 1930s. We know of it only because a member interviewed her friends, wrote up her analysis, and left the manuscript to her partner's daughter, a scholar interested in the history of sexuality.[43] Twenty-five women, all of them white, educated, and middle-class and most from Mormon homes, lived discreetly as lesbians in this community. They knew gay men, and together with them many socialized in a bohemian literary club, although they also interacted with heterosexual couples. The main social characteristic that distinguished them from comparable nonlesbian women was that most worked outside the home. Although three were married to men and two were housewives in lesbian relationships, the rest worked as teachers, nurses, waitresses, or secretaries or in other predominantly female jobs.

No doubt the lingering tradition of romantic friendship protected them to some extent from exposure as lesbians. The author of the manuscript, a photographer, lived in the 1920s with a social worker. They made what she described as an "ideal home" and found social acceptance. This was a gendered relationship. One took responsibility for the "male part of the household," the other "delighted" in being a "happy wife at home."[44] Gender differences emerged in other ways as well. Perhaps in part because the author was much influenced by the sexologists' ideas about inversion, the manuscript described half of the women in the community as having a masculine build and ten as having a "masculine psychology," meaning interest in sports and preference for feminine women as lovers. In contrast, the gay men these women knew merited disapproval for their "attempts at femininity," their "mincing gait," and their ability and desire to "sew, cook, and keep house."[45]

These lesbian women in Salt Lake City strove for respectability, voicing disapproval of sexual expression. They socialized at home and protected their secret, although several longed for the life of San Francisco and went to bars when they could afford to visit there. When Radclyffe Hall's famous lesbian novel *The Well of Loneliness* appeared in 1928, to great controversy, they shunned the very idea of publicity. Fearing exposure, they lived as conventionally as possible, kept their heads down, and apparently succeeded in avoiding denunciation in a Mormon stronghold.

The life story of Julia Boyer Reinstein, a lesbian born in 1906 who taught school in Deadwood, South Dakota, and Castile, New York, during the 1920s and 1930s complicates the picture of lesbian worlds in the years before the Second World War. For Boyer Reinstein lived as a lesbian among lesbian friends, did not hide her relationships from her family, yet did not name or talk about her sexual identity or publicly reveal her interest in women. She was "out," but only in private, with her lovers, suggesting how differently some lesbian communities developed in contrast to public male worlds.[46]

Boyer Reinstein was the daughter of divorced parents, and when her father first reconnected with her when she was in college, he recognized right away that she was a lesbian. In 1928 she went to live with him in Deadwood, where he had had great financial success. She threw herself into affairs with women when she traveled with her father. Amazingly, when she went out to nightclubs with him and his business associates, she would always find a woman with whom she would have sex. (He too always seemed to find willing female partners.) "Invariably, there was a lesbian among them . . . . I would team up with her."[47] Some of them were married, some not. About one, Boyer Reinstein commented, "She was very much a lady. You would never have known it to look at her that she was a lesbian. Never known it—until she went to bed."[48]

Boyer Reinstein also flirted with and engaged in sexual relationships with young women at home in Deadwood, but it was not until she fell in love with another teacher and formed a serious relationship that she felt she had found a truly supportive lesbian world. She and her partner Dorothy became friends with what she called an "odd" couple, the daughter of a local doctor and the masculine female friend she had brought home with her from college. These friends had set up housekeeping together and ran a hair salon, where they put in a sauna and began sponsoring a women's afternoon one day a week.

Such a world could exist, as in Salt Lake City, because the women "were not too obvious," because they were "respectable," and because they had families to protect them. Boyer Reinstein commented that the doctor's daughter's partner was "too obvious, almost," so "there were eyebrows raised" when she first arrived in Deadwood.[49] Boyer Reinstein suspected that people "talked about us behind our backs" and noted that her mother occasionally got upset over snide comments. But on the whole everyone—including the women living with woman lovers—ignored the existence of lesbianism even though they knew about it. These lesbians themselves never talked about it—not only to show that they could be trusted to keep quiet in public, but also because they liked their ambiguous status and had no desire to be publicly labeled a "kind of person." But failing to call themselves lesbians, in either private or public conversation, did not change the fact that they found erotic and emotional satisfaction in their relationships with women.

These peeks into private lesbian worlds—afforded only because of the accident of an inherited manuscript and the good fortune of a willing interviewee—suggest that all over the country there were women and men living in same-sex relationships and building worlds that supported them in their love and desire. Mary Casal, whom we have met as the pseudonymous author of an autobiography published in 1930, told of a series of same-sex relationships from her upstate New York girlhood on, culminating in her love for a woman she called Juno. Casal and Juno believed that "we were the only ones in the world who cherished such a love" until an actress who sometimes played male roles introduced them to "a most astonishing personality—a little woman with short, black hair tinged with gray, wearing heavy white silk pajamas, smoking, and very hospitable."

She looked us through, and I knew at once that she too knew! . . . At last, and too late, did I find that I was not a creature apart as I had always felt. How much suffering would have been saved me and what a different life I would have led if I had known earlier that we are not all created after one pattern nor according to any set rules, but that each is as "normal" as any other![50]

Experiencing the same joy at discovering, through the work of Edward Carpenter, that he was not alone, a Detroit man gave thanks. Writing Carpenter in 1921 for freeing him from "the limitations of my hitherto paradoxical and inexplicable nature," from the "long cruel years" of "the most rigid state of repression," this man put into words what same-sex love and desire meant to him:

Oh what a sweet and sacred thing it is to love and to be loved!—to hold within one's arms the visible representation of that beautiful spark which daily seems to grow brighter and more wondrous, to remove one's thoughts from the realm of self and let them dwell rapturously and selflessly upon some beloved companion, to press his glorious body close to one's own, to feel the warm, red blood pulsing deliciously through both, to feel his soft arms lie caressingly about one's shoulders, to pillow one's head upon his breast, to touch one's lips to his hair, his eyes, his lips! Is Paradise more wonderful?[51]

Similarly, Jeb Alexander, living in Washington in the 1920s in a circle of friends who shared his same-sex desires, described a day of picnicking on the cliffs below Great Falls with his beloved Dash:

We wandered the woods, observing the flowers and trees and climbing rocks. I am passionately in love with Dash. I believe that if I could have him with me I could be happy the rest of my life on a desert isle. Just the two of us alone. I feel that I should like to be father, mother, brother, wife, friend, and lover to him all at the same time.[52]

If the fairies of the big cities led the way in constructing a public homosexual persona, they were not the only ones building communities.

The lesbian worlds of Deadwood and Salt Lake City may have been a far cry from the cruising grounds of Newport, the Near North Side and South Side of Chicago, the Bowery, Greenwich Village, Harlem, or the Boston Public Garden, but in all these locales, as well as in cities and towns across the country, individuals with same-sex desires were finding each other and forming communities. Depending on a whole raft of factors, but especially class, they defined themselves in different ways, marking their gendered presentation, their preferences for particular sexual acts, and their desire for same-sex love and intimacy. Like the "straight" men of Newport or the "wolves" of New York, married middle-class women might have sex with a woman like Julia Boyer Reinstein yet not think of themselves as lesbians. The association between sexual acts and identity was complex, contradictory, and changing. The work of the sexologists might have had an impact on those, like Jeb Alexander, who read Havelock Ellis and took on themselves the concept of "inversion," but many different ideas about same-sex sexual acts rubbed metaphorical shoulders in the bustling streets of urban neighborhoods.

In a variety of locales, middle-class men and women seemed to shun public expressions of a "gay" or "lesbian" identity. Samuel Kent and Arthur Green in Newport differentiated between their "Christian Brotherhood" and queer desire. Middle-class men in New York embraced the term "queer" but rejected fairy effeminacy as too visible and too vulgar. Middle-class women in Salt Lake City and Deadwood emphasized respectability and discretion, in contrast to the cross-dressed working-class women in Chicago and New York who ventured into bars and dance halls.

All these different kinds of communities depended on access to social spaces, whether the Long Beach Bathhouse, the YMCA, the Michigan Avenue bridge, "fairy resorts," drag balls, rent parties, street corners, bohemian restaurants, private homes, or the sauna in Deadwood on "ladies' afternoon." The existence of heterosexual bohemian or artistic communities served as the wedge for men and women seeking same-sex contacts. From the artistic world of Greenwich Village to the institutions of the Harlem Renaissance to the bohemian literary club of Salt Lake City, gay men and lesbians built new worlds alongside heterosexual women and men experimenting with social and sexual freedoms. And in this context, people with different sexual desires mixed far more easily than we might expect.

Much of this activity—the formation of different kinds of identities and the building of diverse same-sex communities—was new in the early twentieth century. Yet the salience of gender differences for the expression of same-sex sexuality, so crucial in the past, remained. The fairies who took women's names, the queer men camping it up in their private lives, the working-class women in men's clothes, and the middle-class lesbian housewives all continued to associate their sexual desires with gendered appearances and behaviors. In this sense these early twentieth-century communities sat on the cusp of old and new ways of expressing same-sex desire.

Six

BECOMING A PEOPLE: LESBIAN AND GAY WORLDS AND THE ORGANIZATION OF RESISTANCE

Although I have considered myself "out" for many years—after all, I taught and wrote about the history of same-sex sexuality, I was active in Columbus's gay and lesbian movement, and I was completely open everywhere about my relationship with Verta—until 1993 I had never told my parents I was a lesbian. They were in their eighties, in some ways very unworldly, and they totally accepted that I had chosen to live my life with Verta. (Remember, they had the model of Aunt Leila and Diantha.) I thought it was possible that they "knew," but I didn't really think so.

What prompted me to come out to them was that a reporter from the *New York Times,* in pursuit of a story about generations of lesbians on campus, called to arrange interviews with Verta and me. Apparently she had been to

Wellesley College, where it seemed that practically half the students were proudly and openly lesbian. When she reported on this visit to her boss, he said, "Go to Ohio State." So come to Columbus she did, presumably in search of the real world.

So here I was, faced with the possibility that someone would read the article and say to my parents something like, "I read about Leila in the *Times*." The truth is I would have taken that chance, so sure was I that it wouldn't happen, but Verta convinced me that I couldn't just ignore it, that I had to come out to them.

And so I did. I wrote them a letter, telling them about the forthcoming story and describing what I hoped was my irrational fear that they would reject me, that it would ruin our relationship. I asked my brother, who wasn't the least surprised when I came out to him, to take it to them. I guess I was afraid they might have heart attacks or something. "Part of the reason I haven't felt a compelling need to tell you before is that you already know that I love and have chosen to live my life with a woman, whatever words you may have put on it," I wrote.

From this distance I can barely believe now how hysterical and scared I was after I sent off the letter. But my parents were terrific. They called to say that they loved me, that nothing had changed. I felt enormous relief that I had no more secrets. So I was still happy that I had finally done it when the reporter called to say that her editor was cutting all the material on lesbian faculty, making what was supposed to be a story about generational differences into a story about the students. I sent the article to my parents anyway, and later that summer we talked about it a little bit. My father brought up Aunt Leila but quickly dismissed the thought that she might have been a lesbian. Then he wanted to know whether being a feminist and going to a women's college had made me a lesbian.

CHAPTER SIX

This is a thoroughly modern story—with its media-inspired crisis, the emphasis on coming out, and the role of the lesbian and gay movement in both provoking the reporters' interest and inspiring my own delayed announcement—and yet there are threads that we can follow back in time as well. That my father thought about but rejected the comparison to Aunt Leila suggests the tangled relationship of Boston marriage to contemporary lesbianism. That he took a social constructionist position (without having any idea what that might be) on the question of why I was a lesbian, in contrast to Verta's mother, who assured us she knew all about the gay gene, suggests the continuing dispute about the making of sexualities. And that my saying the words, "I am a lesbian," took so long and meant so much to me reflects the salience of naming.

Too often we think of twentieth-century events as massive watersheds in the history of same-sex sexuality. Supposedly the Second World War catapulted us into a new era. And the famous riot at the Stonewall Inn in Greenwich Village in 1969, which marks the beginning of "gay liberation," looms large, dividing the decades into "before" and "after" Stonewall. But as we have already seen in considering the early twentieth century, identification, visibility, and community were not entirely novel in the 1940s and 1950s. And there is nothing inevitable about the shape of lesbian and gay life at the end of the century. It is important to remember this as we explore the tumultuous developments since the 1930s.

I begin my consideration here with the mixed impact of the Second World War on both women and men and the consequences of the McCarthyite attack on "homosexual perversion" in the postwar years. Intensified oppression brought terrible hardship, but it also spread the word about homosexuality. I consider how, in the hostile world of the 1950s, gay and lesbian subcultures persisted. I then turn to the complex world of the butch/fem working-class bar culture of the 1940s and 1950s, a striking contrast to the persistence of romantic friendship among middle-class and upper-class women. I end with what was, indeed, an arresting new development: the emergence of a social movement organized around same-sex sexuality. The homophile movement of the 1950s paved the way for organized resistance that eventually took many forms. When political groups succeeded in mobilizing the social worlds that continued to bring together the largest number of gay and lesbian people, they held out the greatest promise. I end, short of the famous Stonewall riot, with small demonstrations and political campaigns—indications that Stonewall is indeed just a handy way of marking a turning point that had been long in the making.

"This Is the Army"

The Second World War holds an important place in the history of same-sex sexuality, having created spaces for the survival and spread of the gay cultures that had flourished in New York and elsewhere in the 1920s. As we have seen, the economic crisis of the 1930s and the accompanying cultural backlash against the social experimentation of the Roaring Twenties pushed gay culture out of the mainstream and more or less out of sight in most places. But America's entrance into the war to some extent reversed that process. Not only did mobilization bring about increased geographical mobility, re-moving soldiers and sailors and women war workers recruited to boom towns from the confines of small-town life, but the sex-segregated nature of both the military and the war industry heightened the chance that individuals with unexpressed or unacknowledged same-sex desires would make contact with others who shared those feelings. Women with access to formerly male jobs in industry experienced a loosening of social and sexual control. Even respectable white middle-class women could socialize in public without men and wear pants publicly without reproach. But, ironically, it was the military that gave the biggest boost to the elaboration of gay culture.

From the very beginning of wartime mobilization in 1941, attempts to eliminate homosexuals from the ranks of fighting men called attention to their existence. As part of the intensified psychological testing designed to improve the mental health of the armed forces, men inducted into the military encountered frank and potentially consciousness-raising questions about their sexual conduct and desires. Homosexual men, the military assumed, were too effeminate to be good soldiers and too mentally unstable to hold up under pressure. Because masculinity suited, rather than un-suited, women for military service, women inductees escaped scrutiny for sexual deviance until near the end of the war, when the mother of a private discovered love letters written to her daughter by a Women's Army Corps sergeant and threat-ened to tell the world that the Corps was "full of homosexuals and sex maniacs."[1] From the first men faced questions about whether they liked girls, if they were homosexual or had had homosexual feelings, or if they had had sex with men or boys. Some gay men lied to get into the service, others told the truth and suffered the consequences. Psychiatrist interviewers, trained by the Selective Service, watched for bodily discomfort or effeminate physical characteristics in naked selectees or pricked up their ears at questions such as, "Why do I get embarrassed with women? . . . Why have I been approached by so many 'fairies?' "[2] What this process meant was that every man inducted into the armed forces had to classify his sexuality and confront the possibility of homosexual feelings or experiences.

Despite the best efforts of the psychiatrists, the new screening process did not, in fact, keep confirmed or potential gay men out of the service. For a variety of reasons—because men who already identified as gay excelled at hiding their inclinations, because some men did not label their feelings or behavior as "homosexual," because gay military officers looked the other way, and at bottom because eventually any warm body would do—gay men in significant numbers found themselves in the armed forces. Nineteen-year-old New York City draftee Robert Fleischer, desperate to get into the army, enthusiastically proclaimed his liking for girls in 1943 and made it in. "My God, couldn't he see my curly platinum hair that was partly bleached, the walk, maybe the sissy S in my voice?" he wondered.[3]

With no formal screening procedures in place for women, lesbians flocked to the military. Pat Bond, who enlisted in 1945, described the officer at the recruiting station as looking "sort of like all my old gym teachers in drag. Stockings, little earrings, her hair slicked back and very daintily done so you couldn't tell she was a dyke, but *I* knew!"[4] Yet the military brass were not unconcerned about lesbianism. Rumors about the sexual immorality of the Women's Army Corps—spread by servicemen and not, as the military feared, by German spies—hampered recruitment efforts, leading to tightened screening procedures as the war progressed. Women's Army Corps recruiters began to inquire about enlistees' motivations for joining up, asking if they wanted to "be with other girls."[5] Throughout the war, the WAC leadership hoped to suppress lesbianism without calling public attention to the problem, so what might look like tolerance was in reality an attempt to protect the fragile reputation of the Corps.[6]

Once in, men found themselves in an all-male environment that fostered bonding between "buddies" and threw men together in tents, beds, and train berths. Gay men could find ways to have sex if they dared. As in Newport during the First World War, even heterosexual men might engage in same-sex acts, as long as they did the penetrating, without feeling any stigma. Lesbians in the military tended to pair off, drawing attention, according to one observer, only if they always hung out together, shared a cigarette, kissed lingeringly, or called each other "darling" or "sweetheart."[7] Yet increasing fear for the reputation of the Women's Army Corps provoked investigations that targeted any woman with a masculine "haircut . . . manner of wearing clothing . . . posture . . . or stride" or any woman trying to "date other girls such as a man would."[8]

Despite official disapproval of homosexuality in the military, gay women and men found themselves sometimes tolerated in the interests of the war effort and able to fit into special roles. Astonishingly, psychiatrists advised Women's Army Corps officers that they could mold "potential homosexual tendencies" into strong admiration for a woman leader that would produce an exemplary soldier.[9] Cross-gender occupations—motor transport for women, secretarial work or nursing for men—made a place for butch women and "sissy" men, though African American women in the Women's Army Corps had to fight to stay out of the most menial service jobs. Even extremely effeminate men could play the barracks "fairy," a comic role familiar to many from the 1920s "pansy craze." All-male (and racially segregated) shows that soldiers put on for the troops gave some men the chance to dress in drag. Army Special Services put out handbooks with scripts, music, lyrics, set designs, and even dress patterns. Performing in drag for one's buddies was not without its dangers, despite the long tradition of men in sex-segregated cultures dressing up as women as an ironic way of affirming their masculinity. The crackdown on female impersonation in the 1930s had associated drag more firmly with homosexuality and perversion, so soldier drag queens had to walk a fine line.[10]

Off base, gay men and women sought out institutions where they could socialize, giving an enormous boost to the gay bar. Traditional sites such as private parties increasingly gave way to public commercialized forms of entertainment suited to a young, large, and geographically mobile population. From the rare lesbian bars such as Mona's in San Francisco and the If Club and Lakeshore Club in Los Angeles to the posh hotel bars for men at the Astor in New York, the Mark Hopkins in San Francisco, and the Biltmore in Los Angeles to the interracial public drag balls at Finnie's Club in Chicago and Phil Black's Fun Makers Club in Harlem, military women and men, whether middle or working class, white or of color, could find a place to be themselves. Wartime mobility spread the news of choice locations and disseminated gay slang across the country, helping to nationalize lesbian and gay subcultures. Sometimes the military police, concerned with fighting vice and especially venereal disease, even served as a source of information about the gay life by posting certain establishments as off-limits.[11]

If wartime mobilization fostered a boom in lesbian and gay subcultures, above all in San Francisco, the port of departure for and arrival from the Pacific theater of war, life in the military was not all fun, games, and drag shows for gay service personnel. Unable to imprison all homosexual offenders, the military, prompted by psychiatrists, instituted the system of dishonorable discharges (known as "blue discharges" because they were printed on blue paper) for homosexuals during the war. Only criminal offenders who committed same-sex rape or had sex with a minor would be imprisoned. Those classified as "true" or "confirmed" homosexuals who engaged in consensual sex would be discharged. And "normal young men," not "by nature homosexuals" but who "submitted

GI drag shows during the Second World War: "This Is the Army" and "Jumping with Jodie." Army Signal Corps Photograph Collection, 111-SC-1405222 and 111-SC-208040. Courtesy of the National Archives, Washington, D.C.

to the practice" because drunk or curious would be "rehabilitated and retained," so great was the nation's need in wartime.[12] This supposedly more humane system, based on the paternalistic pity introduced by the medical reformers at the turn of the century, not incidentally increased the power of the psychiatric profession. And the new system, despite the rejection of across-the-board legal sanctions, enhanced the military's system of surveillance and punishment of homosexuals. Listen to the interrogation of a woman corporal accused of a sexual relationship with a woman lieutenant:

Q. What do you do when you and Lt. Foster get together and make love?

A. We just love each other.

Q. How? Describe it to me.

A. We put our arms around each other and love each other . . . .

Q. Have you ever touched her sexual organs?

A. No ma'am.

Q. What physical reaction do you get from kissing Lt. Foster and petting her?

A. I would say I get the same reaction that I would get from kissing a man . . . .

Q. Have you ever heard the term "to come" expressed—meaning someone has been relieved physically, that one has had a physical reaction as a result of being made love to?

A. Yes ma'am.

Q. How do you love one another to get this reaction?

A. We are very close to each other . . . .

Q. Did you learn it from her?

A. I think we learned it together . . . .

Q. We are here to eliminate from the Army people who practice this kind of thing. If you know anything about these kinds of people . . . we want you to tell us.

A. . . . Do I have to drag other people into this?[13]

Approximately ten thousand GIs, all but a few dozen of them men, found themselves interrogated about their sex lives and lovers, locked up on psychiatric wards, publicly humiliated and abused, and eventually discharged with a stain on their records they could never erase.

The war had complex consequences for people with same-sex desires. Gay veterans who survived in the military came home more aware of gay life and identity. But military service also raised real dangers of exposure and punishment.

Surviving the Postwar Purges

In an increasingly hostile postwar environment, those with blue discharges found themselves denied GI benefits and access to many jobs. Marty Klausner, a gay GI with a dishonorable discharge who ran into one roadblock after another in his attempts to find work and get schooling in Pittsburgh, wrote to a friend in 1946, "I'm terrifically unhappy and am constantly in a state of utter confusion as to what to do and where to turn."[14] A woman dishonorably discharged from Wright-Patterson Air Force Base in Ohio nevertheless counted her blessings because she had an understanding family. In contrast, "Two of the girls discharged for homosexuality have committed suicide and one other has disappeared completely," she reported.[15]

From the military, antihomosexual policies spread to the civilian sector of government. In the tense atmosphere of the Cold War, with its glorification of the nuclear family as a bastion against communism, gay men and lesbians lost jobs in government with devastating personal consequences. Senator Joseph McCarthy, with his trusty (and, ironically, gay) aide Roy Cohn at his side, linked communist subversion with "homosexual perversion." A 1950 Senate committee report titled *Employment of Homosexuals and Other Sex Perverts in*

Government concluded that even one pervert "tends to have a corrosive influence upon his fellow employees. These perverts will frequently attempt to entice normal individuals to engage in perverted practices. This is particularly true in the case of young and impressionable people who might come under the influence of a pervert."[16] *New York Daily Mirror* columnist Lee Mortimer wrote a series of lurid exposés reporting that lesbians formed cells in schools and universities and wormed their way into the armed forces, where they seduced and even raped their innocent peers. In the government "10,000 faggots"—"people you wouldn't let in your garbage wagon"— had infiltrated, with dire results.[17] Dismissals from all levels of government service increased, and countless lesbians and gay men never made it through the new screening processes designed to keep them out in the first place.

Even if they avoided government or military service, gay men and lesbians could not assume they would be safe. A nationwide panic about "sexual psychopaths" increased fears of "deviants," including homosexuals. When news of a sex crime hit the papers, police often cracked down on male homosexuals, regardless of the facts of the case. After the murder of a child in Chicago in 1946, Marty Klausner, the gay GI quoted above, wrote to a friend: "I suppose you read about the kidnapping and killing of the little girl in Chicago— I noticed tonight that they 'thought' (in their damn self righteous way) that perhaps a pervert had done it and they rounded up all the females [gay men]—they blame us for everything."[18]

Furthermore, the Federal Bureau of Investigation, headed by the infamously closeted J. Edgar Hoover, gathered records of morals arrests from local police departments, scoured newspapers for articles about the gay subculture, compiled information about gay bars, and infiltrated the early homosexual rights organizations. Post office officials instituted surveillance of men who subscribed to physique magazines and other publications popular with gay men and even joined gay pen-pal clubs to try to trace networks of "deviants." Raids on lesbian and gay bars and gay male cruising spots increased, and newspapers routinely printed the names and addresses of those caught up in the sweeps. Police arrested sixty-three women in a single raid in New Orleans in 1953.[19] In Boise, Idaho, in 1955, the arrest of three men accused of having sex with teenage boys led to a fifteen-month investigation that involved questioning 1,400 residents.[20] A Florida legislative committee headed by conservative state senator Charley Johns launched an investigation in 1958 of homosexual activity at the University of Florida. Paying precious little attention to legal niceties, the Johns Committee questioned witnesses, publicized charges based on hearsay, and eventually dismissed sixteen members of the faculty and staff. All, not coincidentally, were involved in the civil rights movement, confirming the conclusion of the Florida Civil Liberties Union that sexual morality was not the real or only issue in this investigation.[21]

Although such assaults took their toll, heightened wartime expectations led in the immediate postwar years to an early attempt to win justice for homosexuals. Launched by black civil rights advocates who pointed to the racist use of dishonorable discharges against African American soldiers who had ventured to protest their racially unfair treatment, a campaign against the punitive discharge measures included homosexual veterans as " 'unfortunates' of the Nation preyed upon by the blue discharge."[22] Some gay veterans even dared to speak out publicly on their own behalf. A discharged Women's Army Corps officer wrote anonymously in 1945 to *Yank,* the army weekly, pointing out, "Many Army medical doctors believe strongly concerning the injustice of this situation. If only people would realize this and help us with understanding rather than casting us out with condemnation!"[23]

Veteran Henry Gerber, who as early as the 1920s tried to organize homosexuals, asked the director of the Mental Hygiene Bureau in Washington, "Shall these thousands of homosexuals who fought in this war have come back to this country to find that they fought in vain and that persecution of them is still going on as before in this land of ours, disgraced by the presence of stupid and hypocritical fanatics?"[24] During a brief period of tolerance some homosexuals won upgrades of their discharges. But in 1947, when army hard-liners replaced most dishonorable discharges with general discharges, nothing changed in the case of homosexuals, who remained "undesirable" and, reversing wartime policy, became "unreclaimable" as well.

But the witch-hunts in the military and civilian life did not succeed in destroying the existing subcultures. As in the case of the armed forces' screening process, public discussion of the "homosexual menace" spread word of the gay life. This meant that it was easier to find not only for the hostile observers but also for those seeking such a life.

Places to Go

Despite the forces of oppression unleashed against those with same-sex desires in the Cold War years, sources of information on homosexuality multiplied and enclaves of acceptance persisted or opened up in a variety of places. Alfred Kinsey's famous studies *Sexual Behavior in the Human Male,* published in 1948, and *Sexual Behavior in the Human Female,* which followed in 1953, presented the shocking finding that far more white Americans (Kinsey included information only about his white subjects) engaged in same-sex sexual relations than was commonly believed. With his characteristic statistical precision, Kinsey stated that 37 percent of white males and 13 percent of white females had had orgasms with someone of the same sex, and 50 percent of white men and 28 percent of white women had had some kind of "homosexual response."[25] Although Kinsey sought to break down the notion that people could be divided into two rigid categories of "heterosexual" and "homosexual," his seven-point continuum from exclusive heterosexuality to exclusive homosexuality did not really accomplish that. But he certainly caught and held the attention of Americans, whose eyes were opened to a far wider variety of sexualities than they had previously acknowledged.

Along with the Kinsey reports, an explosion of books and magazines brought homosexuality into the public arena. Lesbian pulp novels appeared on the shelves of corner drugstores. Mostly written by male authors for a heterosexual audience, such inexpensive paperbacks depicted lesbian life as pathetic and unhappy. Even the stories written by lesbian authors, who were more likely to depict strong and admirable heroines, generally had to end unhappily. Yet lesbian readers treasured these books, since at least women loved and desired other women within their covers. Imagine what it might have been like for a lesbian to read the following passage, even if the novel ended with Laura bravely giving up her sorority sister Beth to heterosexuality:

"Mmmm . . . . " Beth murmured as Laura's hands began to trace the curves of her back. "Oh, that's marvelous." She shivered a little and Laura trembled with her. "Under my pajamas, Laur." . . . And Laura's hands descended to their enthralling task again, caressing the flawless hollows, the sweet shoulders. She was lost to reason now . . . . A wash of heat flooded Laura's face. She bent over Beth and began to kiss her like a wild, hungry child, pausing only to murmur, "Beth, Beth, Beth . . . . " Beth rolled over on her back then and looked up at Laura, reaching for her, breathing hard and smiling a little, and her excitement consumed the last of Laura's reserve. Her lips found Beth's, and found them welcoming.[26]

Gay men could read their own pulp novels or choose from the burgeoning male physique magazines that the Supreme Court had declared were not obscene. Serious literature, too, such as Jean Genet's *Our Lady of the Flowers,* James Baldwin's *Another Country,* William Burrough's *Naked Lunch,* and Mary McCarthy's *The Group* included gay and lesbian characters. Even Hollywood, where film producers had since 1930 adhered to a code that banned "sex perversion," began cautiously to explore same-sex sexuality in the early 1960s in such films as *The Children's Hour* and *Advise and Consent.*[27]

The "beat" scene of the 1950s, too, like earlier avant-garde artistic subcultures, called attention to homosexuality and created a space within cafés and coffeehouses where gay life flourished. The North Beach section of San Francisco became the center of an artistic movement that rejected the conformity and consumerism of the Cold War era and instead celebrated sexual experimentation and social protest. Allen Ginsberg's *Howl,* a poem in the tradition of Walt Whitman, made North Beach famous when in 1957 the police confiscated copies and arrested bookstore owner Lawrence Ferlinghetti for selling obscene literature. Journalists denounced the beats as "young hedonists who don't really care whether something is good or evil, as long as it is enjoyable" and as "poets, pushers, and panhandlers, musicians, male hustlers, and a few marginal esthetes seeking new marginal directions."[28] When police raided a coffeehouse in normally staid Philadelphia in 1959, the escalating conflict pitted the authorities against "men in beards" and "girls in tights." One reporter explained, "The proprietors and habitues say they are college students, artists and art students, persons looking for a quiet place to spend an inexpensive evening in a non-alcoholic atmosphere. Neighbors of the places and policemen add to that list homosexuals, dope users and various types of odd characters."[29]

In yet a different arena, the drag balls that had long served as a central institution of the gay male world reached their peak of popularity and visibility in the immediate postwar years. Although the balls in Chicago and New York attracted both African American and white crowds, it was the black press that reported on them. On the black and working-class South Side of Chicago in the 1950s, Finnie's Ball was the social event of the year. As *Ebony* described the 1952 ball: "The men who don silks, satins and laces for the yearly masquerade are as style-conscious as the women of a social club planning an annual charity affair or a society dowager selecting a debutante gown for her favorite daughter."[30] That the drag balls drew giant crowds and made the pages of the major African American publications at the same time that the military and federal government undertook purges of homosexuals shows that the forces of toleration and oppression always intermingled. And the interest of the larger African American community in the drag balls, although not always entirely positive, suggests that the coexistence of gay and straight worlds (and also perhaps a more fluid notion of sexuality) that characterized urban life early in the twentieth century may have lingered longer in some communities than in others.

Another, very different community that bucked the trend of the antihomosexual 1950s was Cherry Grove on Fire Island, New York. Gay theater people had first discovered Cherry Grove in the 1930s, and in the postwar years the small, isolated summer community became "like a very private gay country club," according to one insider.[31] "I was free as a bird in the fifties," she added. News of Cherry Grove spread by word of mouth at gay bars or private parties in New York. English poet W. H. Auden and his companion Chester Kallman spent time in Cherry Grove, as did other literary celebrities such as Carson McCullers, Tennessee Williams, and Truman Capote. By the 1950s, newspaper references such as "Cherry Grove, Fire Island's outpost of Greenwich Village," helped to solidify the community's reputation and draw ever more gay and lesbian visitors. As one Grover put it, everyone knew that "this was where gay people could go and have a ball."[32] Like other resorts, this was an exclusive world, open only to white, middle- and upper-class people loosely connected to the world of the arts. Yet its very existence testifies to the oases some people could construct in the face of massive oppression.

Across the country, men and women with same-sex desires sought out places where they could live their lives as freely as possible. San Francisco, already a city with a reputation as wide open to sexual and gender nonconformity, became a sort of gay haven in the postwar years. As a tongue-in-cheek newspaper headline proclaimed in 1949, "HOMO-SEXUALS AND LESBIANS WELCOME TO SAN FRANCISCO—HALF-A-DOZEN CENTERS AVAILABLE FOR YOUR USE—YOU MAY FREQUENT WITHOUT MOLESTATION COUNTLESS THEATERS AND PARKS—WE CATER TO YOUR NEEDS."[33]

But even those who did not end up in the gay capital of San Francisco might find an expanded social scene at home. In the aftermath of the war Washington, D.C., hosted numerous bars, segregated by both race and sex. In the late 1940s cities such as Kansas City, Missouri, Richmond, Virginia, Worcester, Massachusetts, and San Jose, California, boasted gay bars. In addition, public cruising areas for men interested in sex with other men expanded in the postwar years. According to a sensational exposé that inadvertently provided a guide to gay life, Lafayette Square—"Garden of Pansies"—as well as Dupont Circle attracted men looking for men in Washington.[34] If this was not exactly news—remember Jeb Alexander picking up men in the 1920s—the places where gay men might find each other were increasing.

In Flint, Michigan, and surely in other cities as well, the postwar boom in automobile ownership made cars, as well as bars and parks, handy places where men might have sex with other men. At 2:30 on a June morning in 1950, police discovered a cross-dressed twenty-five-year-old African American male employee of Fisher Body having sex in a parked Chevrolet with another man who worked for the power company. Applying an unconsciously ironic term, the court-appointed psychiatrists in the case deemed the man dressed in women's clothes an "active homosexual." The cross-dresser told them that she was "born queer" and that she had "practiced the use of his mouth as a sex organ" since the age of eight. The judge, as a result of the evaluation, committed her to Ionia State Hospital.[35] In Flint, most of the arrests for consensual sodomy in the 1950s resulted when the police found men having sex in cars.

Cars, within financial reach of the auto workers of Flint as well as well-paid working-class men in other cities, also stimulated the growth of more traditional gay gathering places. "Tearooms" sprang up at roadside rest stops across the country, and people in towns without bars could drive to the nearest city.[36] Depending on where they lived, lesbians and gay men in the postwar years might have to decide to leave home and head to a big city to continue "in the life." Or they might, like Birmingham, Alabama, native "Barry Kline," stay home but take advantage of local and longer-distance travel to explore gay worlds.[37] Whatever the method, and despite the dangers, people knew there were places to go.

Butch and Fem in the 1950s: The Heyday of the Lesbian Bar

The war had special consequences for lesbian women because, once it had loosened social conventions for all women, the behavior of lesbians no longer stood out so vividly. Heterosexual women war workers did things that "respectable" women had never done—they went out in public to bars and clubs without male escorts, and they wore pants on the street—normalizing some aspects of lesbian behavior. Although lesbians could be spotted at gay institutions long before the 1940s, specifically lesbian bars opened only as women broke through the social conventions mandating female abstinence from alcoholic beverages and the need for a male escort in public.

Class, race, and ethnicity played important roles in structuring lesbian bar life. In blue-collar Buffalo, New York, the place we know most about, the lesbian bar in the 1940s was primarily the preserve of white working-class women, although the crowd grew more diverse in the 1950s. Upper- and middle-class Buffalo women in the 1940s mostly socialized in posher straight places or at home, but by the 1950s middle-class lesbians could be seen in both lesbian and mixed gay and lesbian bars. In Albuquerque, New Mexico, in the 1960s it was not class but willingness to be "out" about one's sexuality that distinguished bar-going lesbians from those who stayed away, and the two groups sometimes partied and played softball together.[38] Memphis, Tennessee, had no lesbian bars until the 1960s, but lesbians and gay men would go in groups to straight "juke joints" or "mom-and-pop bars" where they felt at home. As in Albuquerque, the softball field also served as closeted lesbian space.[39]

African American and Native American women were welcome only in small numbers at the white bars in Buffalo, yet they lacked their own places. They threw house parties or patronized racially mixed clubs in which heterosexual and homosexual women and men rubbed shoulders. In South Philadelphia in the 1950s, a bar called Jeannette Dembry's had a primarily African American lesbian clientele, whereas specifically African American lesbian bars did not open in Detroit until the 1960s.[40] Black women began to desegregate the bars in Buffalo as the decades wore on, and upwardly mobile lesbians also began to venture out more often, making the lesbian bar community not only more diverse but more racially and class mixed than the larger society.

Finding a lesbian bar could be a momentous occasion. Marla, a black lesbian from Buffalo who had been in the military and who worked as a taxi dispatcher, found out about the lesbian bar Bingo's when she answered a call. "They were surprised that it was a woman at the other end, 'cause men had always been dispatchers . . . . And I started talking to them and found out that the woman on the phone and I had been in the same branch of the service. And then I'm trying to find out where the bar was 'cause I was going to go down and meet them, not knowing what kind of bar I was going to go into right away."[41] For some women, the lesbian bar represented a lifeline. As a woman from Lowell, Massachusetts, described the Moody Gardens in the 1950s, "To us it was our world, a small world, yes; but if you are starving you don't refuse a slice of bread, and we were starving."[42]

The bar culture developed well-defined norms and modes of dress and behavior. Women identified as either "butch" or (the preferred African American term) "stud," or else they were "fem." Not simply a mimicking of heterosexuality, the embracing of different gender styles served as both an erotic statement and a social system. By the 1950s the long tradition of utilizing masculinity as a way of proclaiming sexual interest in women had resulted in a new-style lesbian, the "tough butch." She dressed in typical male working-class attire as much of the time as possible and went to the bar every evening of the week. This set her apart from straight middle-class society, marked her as different, and put well-paying jobs and other privileges out of reach. Fems, who dressed more conventionally, could hold down traditional female jobs but nevertheless announced their sexual identity through their

Butches and fems, ca. 1945. The Buddy Kent Collection.
© LHEF, Inc. Courtesy of the Lesbian
Herstory Archives, Brooklyn, New York.

association with butches. Butch and fem couples, on the
city streets, proclaimed their sexual desires publicly. As one
Buffalo butch described it, "People looked at me a lot . . .
either they weren't sure if I was male or female or I looked
like a lesbian to them . . . and I looked either like a woman
in men's clothes or they didn't know what the hell I was."[43]
Being either butch or fem was imperative. The 1950s community had derogatory terms for women who could not be
consistently characterized as one or the other—"ki-ki" or
"AC/DC"—but even such women confirmed the duality of
the system, for they could only switch between roles, not
combine them.

Butch and fem roles determined an individual's potential sexual partners and structured intimate relationships
between women. The butch or stud was the "doer," whose
primary goal was to give the fem sexual satisfaction. Carried
to its furthest point, this system produced the ideal of the

untouchable or "stone" butch, who never let her lover lay a finger on her. "If I could give her satisfaction to the highest, that's what gave me satisfaction," as a Buffalo stone butch put it.[44] How often stone butches attained the goal of untouchability is open to debate. But certainly the butch/fem system emphasized the pleasure of the fem, thus affirming women's sexuality. As Joan Nestle, who came out as a fem in the 1950s, put it, "We knew what we wanted and that was no mean feat for young women of the 1950s, a time when the need for conformity, marriage and babies was being trumpeted at us by the government's policy makers."[45] Proclaiming oneself butch or fem through dress and behavior determined the universe of potential lovers and partners. Whether for a single sexual encounter or for the serial monogamy that characterized lesbian relationships in the bar culture, butches sought out only fems, and fems only butches.

Bar life was both welcoming and dangerous, and on this tricky terrain lesbians created and fought for public social space for themselves. "Barrooms were a way of life; that's where you were among friends. I think it's a place where you could let your hair down; could really be yourself," a Buffalo woman remembered.[46] Yet lesbian bars were not safe from the incursion of straight men, who might try to pick up a fem or start a fight with a butch. In Detroit, heterosexual couples visited the bars to gawk at the lesbians. "You just got to the point where you, if you wanted to enjoy yourself, you had to ignore them because they really never said anything to you, they would just sit there and be amused. I mean, we were their x-rated, sort of like, back in the fifties, sixties."[47] In the parts of town where lesbian bars were located, lesbians mixed with denizens of the sexual underworld. Some fems worked as prostitutes, hiking up the chances for fights between butches and straight men.

Like drag in the gay male world, butch and fem ways of being challenged mainstream gender roles and created a core identity, even if it was one that changed over time. Just as the male world of the 1920s and 1930s distinguished between "fairies" and "normal" men who might have sex with them, in the bar culture of the 1940s butches were "gay" because of their masculine inclinations and sexual interest in women, while fems often saw themselves as different from heterosexual women only because of their association with butches and their participation in the community. In this context it was not even clear that butches and fems were both "lesbians." This changed by the end of the 1950s, when, as in the male world, same-sex sexual attraction, rather than gender presentation, increasingly became the salient marker of who was "gay." As a butch woman who came out in 1957 while still underage put it, "I knew, before I put a concept or a word to it that I was gay . . . . And I had a friend at the time; we used to talk about how we were different and how we liked girls and we had crushes on girls."[48]

Women in the bar culture made same-sex love and desire publicly visible, and in this way they engaged in a form of everyday resistance. Not only did butch/fem couples affirm women's autonomous sexuality to those who saw them on the streets, but butches challenged traditional expectations of feminine appearance and behavior by dressing publicly in masculine styles and by standing up for—and even physically fighting for—their right to "their" fems and to public space.

The emergence of lesbian bar culture in the postwar years gave a public face to female same-sex sexuality. Not all women who loved other women, of course, would dare to venture into a lesbian bar. But the "sexual courage" of butches and fems made a difference, even for those women who would never have claimed kinship with tough bar lesbians.[49]

The Persistence of Romantic Friendship

Women—especially middle- and upper-class women—continued to form relationships with other women that neither they nor the larger society labeled "lesbian." Well into the twentieth century, women formed couples, made lives together, and expressed their love and erotic longing while they and the world around them could distinguish what they were from "female homosexuals." From the White House in Washington to the Main Line of Philadelphia and to New York's Greenwich Village and San Francisco's Chinatown, romantic friendships lingered alongside the public world of the lesbian bar culture. Consider these cases:

First lady Eleanor Roosevelt was a married woman who moved in a world of respectable but indubitably lesbian women, something that certainly confused those looking in from the outside, both then and now. In the famous passage we have already encountered, the journalist Lorena Hickok wrote to Roosevelt remembering "the feeling of that soft spot just north-east of the corner of your mouth against my lips," and Roosevelt confided her wish to "lie down beside you tonight and take you in my arms." Although Franklin Roosevelt called some of Eleanor's necktie-wearing friends "she-men," Eleanor herself did not transgress the boundaries of respectability enough to merit denunciation by Franklin or anyone else as a lesbian or bisexual woman. How she viewed herself we shall never know, in part because Lorena Hickok burned most of Eleanor's letters after her death. But if we consider Eleanor in context, in her world of coupled women who exchanged pinkie rings and brought each other violets, who reveled in the romance of the closet, we can see that, as with Julia Boyer Reinstein back in Deadwood, it was their respectability, their class privilege, their ladylike pearls, that protected them.[50]

If wealth helped protect Roosevelt from suspicion of deviance, Pauline Newman and Frieda Miller, prominent labor activists, seemed to rely on chutzpah as a form of protection.[51] Newman, who cut her hair short and favored tweeds and ties, was a working-class Jewish organizer for the Women's Trade Union League when in 1917 she met and fell in love with Miller, daughter of a German Protestant mill owner and a research assistant at Bryn Mawr College. Disgusted with academic life, Miller left to work for the Trade Union League in Philadelphia, and the two women became a couple. They formed a tight circle with sister unionists Rose Schneiderman and Maud Swartz, who also lived in an unnamed partnership. When Newman first fell in love with Miller, she turned to the older Schneiderman for advice. Schneiderman responded to "Paul," as Newman called herself:

There must be thousands of women who feel like us, eurning [yearning], eurning all the time for warmth and tenderness from a loved one, only to be worn out and settled down to the commonplace everyday grind. You ask whether one should grasp at the possibility for joy held out to one—Why not? I always feel that whatever I have done, could not be done in any other way because of the kind of personality that I am, and not for any other consideration. . . . What I mean is that if any of my love affairs did not go further than they did it was [not] because of the possible circumstances that might follow but because it just did not happen.[52]

Newman seemed to have found her life's love in Miller, but Miller, torn about making a commitment to Newman, had an affair with a married man and, in 1922, became pregnant. Taking advantage of a trip to an international congress of working women in Vienna, the two women left for Europe, telling their friends that Miller was going to adopt an orphan. When they arrived back in New York with Miller's daughter Elisabeth in tow, the two women settled in to their Greenwich

Village home, proudly displaying pictures of Elisabeth on their desks at work. Together they raised her, Newman continuing in her labor activism and Miller going into high-level government service, including heading the Women's Bureau of the Department of Labor. Their relationship seems to have grown increasingly difficult after the Second World War, when Miller began to travel extensively for the International Labor Organization. Differences of class and ethnic background, as well as what might be considered either personal style or gender, caused more friction over time. Newman was gruff, a "give-them-hell kind of person," whereas the press described "Mother Miller," embroidering during meetings, as "a practical, lovable champion of feminine rights."[53] When Miller had an affair with a man in India in the 1950s, Newman reacted with fury, and the two women had almost no contact for six years. Eventually they reconciled and spent the last years of their lives living together. But Miller insisted to Elisabeth that they were not "lesbians in the conventional sense" and that the relationship was not "fully sexual." Newman threatened to sue a historian who implied that they were lesbians.[54]

And one final example: Margaret Chung, the first American-born woman physician of Chinese descent, famous as "Mother Chung" to thousands of American servicemen during the Second World War, formed romantic attachments with at least two women in the 1930s and 1940s.[55] She met Elsa Gidlow, an openly lesbian poet, in the late 1920s when Gidlow and her lover, Tommy, became Chung's patients. Chung at this time dressed in male clothing and used the name Mike. Gidlow described her attraction to this "striking woman in her late thirties, smartly dressed in a dark tailored suit with felt hat and flat-heeled shoes."[56] Gidlow, in an open relationship with Tommy, courted Chung, who seemed to reciprocate her feelings but was unwilling to go any further. Gidlow's journal describes "a spontaneous kiss on the mouth" from Chung and Chung's positive response to Gidlow's insistent question, "Do you love me?" Yet Chung was cautious. After performing surgery on Gidlow, Chung told her in the recovery room, "You gave me hell this morning for operating on you; and then you asked me if I loved you. There were people around too," suggesting that her reticence came from fear of being labeled deviant.[57] And in fact Bessie Jeong, another Chinese American physician trained in the 1930s, put it bluntly: Chung "was a homo, a lesbian."[58]

Chung broke from Gidlow after this incident and shortly afterward announced her engagement to a man she never married. Gidlow agonized: "Heavens! how I want to see her . . . . Sometimes I could strangle her for the way she torments me: but there is no use thinking of her . . . . but I would give a year—two years of my life to hold her in my arms for half an hour."[59]

During the Second World War, Chung, who had by then refashioned herself as both maternal and feminine, took up an intimate relationship with Sophie Tucker, a famous vaudeville performer. This time Chung seemed to mask whatever erotic attraction she may have felt and to take the role of "pal" or mother. Hanging around with Tucker during her stint in San Francisco, Chung asked, "Did you miss me, last night, Boss? . . . You are an angel to put up with all my shennanigans, . . . and dont [sic] think I dont appreciate it and love you for your own dear self."[60] She signed letters "Your adoring Mom," saved a special bedroom for Tucker, left her romantic and silly good-night notes. When Tucker helped raise money to pay the mortgage on Chung's house, Chung wrote her: "Wish I could run and jump on your lap and put my arms around you and kiss your dear cheeks—or pinch them hard for you—wish you could look into my eyes and see the mute gratitude there . . . . I'm the luckiest person in the world, to

"To Miss Elsa Gidlow, with keenest admiration,"
Margaret Chung, 1927. Courtesy of the Gay and
Lesbian Historical Society of Northern California.

have your friendship! I love you, for sure & for keeps."[61] In this
relationship, lacking Gidlow's up-front lesbian identity and
the resulting erotic possibilities, Chung felt freer to express
her love for Tucker, and no one seemed to think "Mother
Chung" and Tucker, with her bawdy heterosexual stage presence, were lesbians.

These women's diverse stories make it clear that much
had changed by the mid-twentieth century, yet the emergence of an identifiable lesbian culture in working-class bar
communities did not wipe out public acceptance of older-
style coupling between women. Discretion and respectability, aided by economic and other forms of privilege, made
all the difference. Yet there were connections between the
two worlds. Just as in the community of tough bar lesbians

some women living in respectable couples—Lorena Hickok, Pauline Newman, Margaret Chung in the 1920s—took on a masculine persona or style. Cross-dressing continued to cross classes. And of course, however much women in respectable couples pretended differently, they knew about the worlds in which people acted on their same-sex sexual desires. Eleanor Roosevelt hanging out with her lesbian friends, Pauline Newman and Frieda Miller choosing to live in Greenwich Village, Margaret Chung's fascination with and fear of Elsa Gidlow's lesbian sexuality—all of this warns us to avoid making simple assumptions about sexuality and identity even in the mid-twentieth century.

Into the Streets

What was new under the postwar sun was the formation of lasting organizations designed to improve the lives of those who loved and desired people of the same sex. At what was perhaps the height of oppression of people with same-sex desires, they began to fight back. The very idea of organizing had become possible only because of the notion that a variety of people shared something fundamental with others who had similar desires. We have seen this process in the making. By the mid-twentieth century, individuals who had previously identified as "pansies" or "bulldaggers" or "queers" or "butches" began to embrace, often in addition to these other identities, the idea that they all, women and men, masculine and feminine alike, had something in common. That overarching identity served as the basis for a variety of organizations. As we shall see, some groups emphasized the basic similarity of people with same-sex desires to people with mixed-sex passions, while others called attention to difference. These basic divisions, linked to assimilationist strategies ("we're just like you, so treat us that way") and confrontational ("we're here, we're queer, get used to it") ones, continue into the present.

Not that resistance was entirely new: when four Harlem drag queens were convicted in 1928 and sentenced to sixty days in the workhouse, they called out to the arresting officers as they were led away, "Goodbye dearie, thanks for the trip as we'll have the time of our lives."[62] Taking a less campy tack, butches who fought straight men in the bars asserted their right to live and love as they chose. But that such people could organize and fight collectively to improve their situation— that was very much a new concept.

The first ephemeral organizations in the United States took their inspiration from Weimar Germany in the 1920s, which before the Nazis came to power had been home to a vibrant gay and lesbian culture. There the adoption of a "third sex" identity linked women and men and served as the basis of a civil rights organization, the Scientific-Humanitarian Committee. (Another group, all male, known as the Community of the Special, asserted the differentness—indeed, superiority—of men who desired men over both lesbians and heterosexuals.) Henry Gerber, whom we have already met protesting the discharges of veterans after the Second World War, learned about the pioneering German homosexual rights movement while a soldier in the American army of occupation in Germany after the First World War. On his return, in 1924 he founded what he called the Chicago Society for Human Rights. He managed to recruit a few members and publish two issues of a paper before the police arrested him and the other officers of the group. Reflecting the medical views of homosexuality as well as the cherished American tradition of individual rights, the society's declaration of purpose proclaimed that the organization would promote and protect "the interests of people who by reasons of mental and physical abnormalities are abused and hindered in the legal pursuit of happiness which is guaranteed them by the Declaration of Independence."[63]

In 1930 a German émigré, Ernst Klopfleisch, conceived a plan to form a similar organization in New York. Klopfleisch, like Gerber, knew about the German Scientific-Humanitarian Committee and had made plans while still in Germany to turn a summer resort where he worked into a gathering place for "inverts." Klopfleisch (who changed his name to Ernest Elmhurst after arriving in this country) thought that the only place to reach the "inverts" was at the lavish costume balls that drew thousands of participants. "This would be where to take the first step by distributing cards, which could be placed on the tables, announcing the idea of an organization," he wrote to Magnus Hirschfeld, founder of the Scientific-Humanitarian Committee.[64] Then the membership fees of those who joined could be used to rent rooms in a private club; dances could turn an enormous profit. The group never got off the ground, but Klopfleisch's schemes linked political organizing to social worlds in a way that turned out to be prophetic.

Take, for example, the origins of the first enduring group that made up what came to be known as the "homophile movement." The Mattachine Society, born in 1950, was the brainchild of Harry Hay, a member of the Communist Party. In an attempt to find homosexuals with leftist political leanings, Hay and his first recruit took copies of a Communist Party petition against the Korean War to the gay male beaches in Los Angeles, reasoning that anyone willing to sign might be interested in a homosexual rights organization.[65] This plan never panned out, but Hay's personal contacts eventually turned up three more interested men who together founded Mattachine.

In its original secret, cell-like, and hierarchical incarnation, Mattachine was modeled on the Communist Party.

The organization sponsored discussion groups, developed a theory of homosexuals as a cultural minority, fought police harassment, and in 1953 even began to publish a magazine, *One*. Hay's original impulse to recruit in the gay culture cropped up again in 1952, when a Los Angeles police officer entrapped one of Mattachine's founders in a park and charged him with lewd and dissolute behavior. Mattachine members organized what they called the Citizens Committee to Outlaw Entrapment and circulated flyers at gay beaches and bars, in restrooms, and at park benches and bus stops in areas of the city where homosexual men lived. When the jury deadlocked on the case, the district attorney's office dropped the charges, leading to a growth spurt for the Mattachine Society.

But despite Mattachine's growth and spread, its structure, which promoted progressive analysis and militant action, also limited recruitment and made Mattachine extremely vulnerable in the anticommunist climate of the 1950s. In 1953 an internal revolt and the resignation of the original leaders led to a retreat to respectability. No longer asserting the rights of homosexuals as a cultural minority, the new Mattachine insisted that "the sex variant is no different from anyone else except in the object of his sexual expression."[66] The accommodationist strategy won important allies among religious leaders, civil libertarians, psychologists, and attorneys, and the movement continued to fight for basic civil rights. When the Los Angeles postmaster refused to handle copies of *One* in 1954 on the grounds that it was "obscene, lewd, lascivious and filthy," the editors contested the decision all the way to the Supreme Court, which reversed the lower court's decision favoring the postmaster.[67]

The position of the refashioned organization, which included women but was dominated by men, was similar to that of the first national lesbian organization. Daughters of Bilitis, launched in 1955 in San Francisco, had as its original purpose an alternative to the bar scene, which had limited appeal to the four couples who met to form a social club. Del Martin and Phyllis Lyon, the force behind DOB in its early years, encountered the San Francisco branch of Mattachine, which inspired them to make DOB a political organization dedicated to changing public attitudes toward lesbianism. The original group of eight women split in half over the question of DOB's purpose, the working-class women opting to continue developing a social club.

DOB and its publication, the *Ladder*, worked to prove the respectability of lesbians and to win acceptance within mainstream society. In this the organization set itself apart from the most visible lesbians in American society, the butch and fem women who patronized the bars. DOB urged women to adopt "a mode of behavior and dress acceptable to society," and an early issue of the *Ladder* proclaimed: "The kids in fly front pants and with butch haircuts and mannish manner are the worst publicity that we can get."[68] In turn, women in the butch/fem community sometimes had little use for organizations such as Mattachine. Bar lesbians in Buffalo joined the Mattachine Society of the Niagara Frontier when it coalesced, but some withdrew disillusioned. One woman reported challenging a Mattachine member: " 'Well, you tell me what you really want and what you're really fighting for, and if you're fighting for something that I don't already have I'll gladly pay another year's dues and get in.' She said, 'We're fighting to be able to work where you want to.' I said, 'I work where I want to.' She said, 'To be able to live where you want to without harassment.' I said, 'I live where I want to without harassment.' You know, 'To be able to have your neighbors know what you are and not have them . . . 'I said, 'My neighbors know what I am.' "[69] A Native American woman who lived in Los Angeles in the 1950s went to a homophile meeting with some gay male friends and decided "it wasn't for women at my level."[70] Class differences could play a powerful role in dividing the lesbian world.

Despite the differences between DOB and the bar culture, some women bridged the two sides. The first homophile activists in Philadelphia were middle-class white lesbians who had been part of the bar culture of the 1950s. Likewise in Cincinnati, a woman involved in homophile organizing in the 1960s hung out in the bars with gay men, "rough" lesbians, and bisexual women.[71]

The gay male world, which had a long history of eroticizing class differences, had more success in bridging the chasm between the culture and the movement. Gay bars in San Francisco in the early 1960s served as the source of political mobilization. As in Greenwich Village and Harlem in an earlier decade, the bohemian culture of the North Beach section of San Francisco—the home of what become known as "beat" culture—fostered both sexual experimentation and political radicalism. José Sarria, who performed in drag at the Black Cat bar in North Beach, ran for city supervisor in 1961, and in 1962 the proprietors and employees of several of the city's gay bars formed the Tavern Guild to fight police harassment. Yet it was not always so easy to mobilize men in the bars. In New York, Mattachine member Randy Wicker carried homophile movement literature on his cruising rounds in the bars and met with little success. " 'There's Miss Mattachine,' they would say. They didn't want to hear about it. They would give you arguments: 'We don't want people to know we [look like] everybody else. As long as they think everyone's a screaming queen with eyelashes, we're safe.' "[72] Yet in general the male homophile movement built sturdier bridges to traditional gay male life in the bars and on the streets.

In contrast to the more-or-less separatist politics of the national scene, where Del Martin of the Daughters of Bilitis angrily pointed out men's failure to recognize that lesbians "are not satisfied to be auxiliary members or second class homosexuals," gay women and men sometimes worked together.[73] In 1957 a member of the Ell Club in blue-collar Bridgeport, Pennsylvania, wrote to the *Ladder* to tell how the club had been formed "for the purpose of bringing closer unity between the boys and girls . . . . We abide by the fact that we are all working for one goal, to be accepted."[74] Although the Ell Club never did become part of the burgeoning homophile movement, its goal of unity foreshadowed developments in nearby Philadelphia, where the first homophile activists, as we have seen, were middle-class white lesbians who moved in mixed-sex social worlds. When the Mattachine Society of Philadelphia was organized in 1961, it had a lesbian president and other women among the leaders and members. Later that year the national Mattachine Society, plagued with financial woes, cut ties with all local chapters, and the Philadelphia group took on a new name, the Janus Society. Like both Mattachine and DOB, the Janus Society pursued a strategy of respectability, but it did so as a group of both women and men. After the demise of the Janus Society, Philadelphia's Homophile Action League continued the pattern of lesbian leadership and mixed membership.[75]

It is easy enough to find fault with the homophile movement for its accommodationist tactics, but it is important to remember just how much it meant that members felt no need to apologize for being gay or lesbian. The parallel story of Bayard Rustin, an African American pacifist and civil rights activist in this period, is instructive. Rustin, born in 1912 in the Quaker community of West Chester, Pennsylvania, could have been one of the leftist gay men recruited by Harry Hay on the beaches of Los Angeles, except that he had broken with the Communist Party in 1941 when ordered to give up his work for racial justice.[76] But Rustin threw his energies instead into groups working for peace and civil rights, where his sexuality persistently caused him trouble. His colleagues' knowledge of his desire for young white men troubled his years at the Christian pacifist Fellowship of Reconciliation. When he was arrested in a parked car (shades of Flint!) with two other men in Pasadena in 1953 and sentenced to sixty days for lewd vagrancy, the Fellowship of Reconciliation dismissed him. For his mentor, A. J. Muste, the issue was not same-sex sexuality but promiscuity. He had earlier written to Rustin: "No one, *no one,* has any business being self-righteous—but to *ourselves* we do apply standards and there are *some limits* to self-indulgence, to lying, to being the play-boy, for those who undertake to arouse their fellows to moral issues . . . . if thy right hand offend thee, cut it off."[77] And things never got any easier. Rustin found a home in the War Resisters' League and later the Southern Christian Leadership Conference, in which he played a leading but backstage role as an adviser to Martin Luther King Jr., but talk of his sexuality continued to hound him. Attacked by both Harlem congressman Adam Clayton Powell and South Carolina senator Strom Thurmond (armed by no less than notorious FBI director J. Edgar Hoover), in his courageous and troubled career Rustin reminds us what it meant that some organizations took same-sex desire for granted.

Ironically, perhaps, the civil rights movement and eventually the New Left inspired a new militancy in Mattachine, DOB, and Janus. When the homophile groups of New York, Philadelphia, and Washington joined together in 1963 to form a coalition known as ECHO (East Coast Homophile Organizations), forces both within and outside these groups began to veer away from the politics of assimilation and respectability. As early as 1964 we can see the origins of the sexual, in-your-face, gay male political style that would later flourish in the gay liberation movement of the 1970s. The new male president of Philadelphia's Janus Society advertised his planned publication, *Drum,* as a place for "news for 'queers,' and fiction for 'perverts.' "[78] With photographs of male nudes, irreverent comic strips and fiction, and openness about sex, *Drum* represented a very different kind of gay activism. Once launched, *Drum* quickly outstripped all other homophile publications, gaining a circulation of fifteen thousand.

As the 1960s drew to a close, homophile activism had taken on a variety of faces. One faction clung to the older strategy of "we're just like you." Some within this group adopted new militant tactics, such as picketing. Another faction, represented by *Drum,* celebrated sexuality and embraced a gay aesthetic based on difference from heterosexuality. In considering the diversification of the homophile movement, it is important to remember that all these tendencies had deep roots in same-sex communities.

The moment that typically defines the beginning of the contemporary gay and lesbian movement is the Stonewall riot. But it was not the homophile leadership or the publishers of gay publications who fought the police in the famous raid in 1969. Butches and drag queens claimed the spotlight that night. And it is important to remember that this was hardly the first militant gay protest in the nation's history. In 1963 Randy Wicker, an inveterate homophile activist, led a picket line at the Whitehall Induction Center, protesting the violation of draft record confidentiality of homosexuals. Two years later a tiny contingent in respectable dresses (for women) and ties (for men) marched in Washington, D.C., carrying signs proclaiming "Homosexuals Should Be Judged as Individuals" and "Support Homosexual Rights."[79] On July 4 of that same year, and in "Annual Reminders" staged for the following four years, protesters demonstrated at Independence Hall in Philadelphia as a reminder that the Declaration of Independence had not brought freedom to all.[80] In 1967 brutal police raids on bars in Los Angeles provoked a demonstration on Sunset

Boulevard.[81] Such manifestations make it clear that Stonewall was only a matter of time.

It is impossible to understand either the rapid growth of gay and lesbian cultures or the burgeoning of gay and lesbian organizing without acknowledging the contradictory forces that made homosexuality a more public subject in the second half of the twentieth century. From wartime questioning to McCarthyite denunciations, from the Kinsey reports to such incidents as the 1955 protest against naming the new bridge spanning the Delaware River at Philadelphia after Walt Whitman, it was becoming harder and harder to ignore the existence of men who loved men and women who loved women.[82]

Same-sex communities in the bars and elsewhere gave rise to—at the same time that they sometimes spurned—the early organizations of lesbians and gay men who determined to fight for social recognition, acceptance, and legal rights. The kernel of the idea of an organization of people who loved and desired others of the same sex came from the pioneering efforts in Germany, but until the 1950s American soil proved unable to nurture the tender shoots planted by Henry Gerber and Ernst Klopfleisch. Then the Mattachine Society, with roots in the Communist Party, and the Daughters of Bilitis took hold and began to grow. With the model of civil rights activism before their eyes (despite the civil rights movement's own less than tolerant attitude to same-sex sexuality), gay men and lesbians came together, sometimes working for assimilation into the mainstream and sometimes proudly asserting their difference.

But as we have seen, it was not just the middle-class lesbians who donned dresses to march on picket lines or the gay men in suits who challenged the psychiatric definition of homosexuality who were doing politics in the 1950s and 1960s. The butch bar lesbians who slugged it out with straight men in the streets and the drag queens who dared to flaunt their finery in public were also engaged in acts of political resistance that forever changed the nature of sexual politics in American society. Without the long history of same-sex cultures and communities—and without the intensified oppression of the postwar years—there would have been no movement.

Seven

CONCLUSION: SOMETHING OLD,

SOMETHING NEW

Perhaps it is fitting to end in a place with a historic gay community: Key West. In January 1998 Verta and I happened into the 801 Bar in the middle of a drag show. We quickly realized that this was no ordinary performance, for these were not men impersonating women in any simple sense of the word. These drag queens dressed as women, but they constantly reminded the audience that they were men by referring to how they had tucked their penises, by brandishing dildos, and by miming sexual acts with various audience members. (With men, they acted out gay male sex acts; with women, they became lesbians.) At the end of the show Margo performed "I Am What I Am," from *La Cage aux Folles,* and at the conclusion of the song she removed her wig; then R. V. Beaumont lip-synched a haunting melody, recorded by Charles Aznavour and performed at the New York drag festival "Wigstock," called "What Makes a Man a Man?" It tells the story of a drag queen:

> At night I work in a strange bar
> Impersonating every star
> I'm quite deceiving.
> The customers come in with doubt
> And wonder what I'm all about
> But leave believing.
> I do a very special show
> Where I am nude from head to toe
> After stripteasing.
> Each night the men look so surprised
> I change my sex before their eyes
> Tell me if you can
> What makes a man a man?

R. V. sat at a mirror and began removing her wig, makeup, falsies, and women's clothes. By the last refrain of "Tell me if you can / what makes a man a man?" he had stripped down to his underwear and put on jeans and a T-shirt. He reminded the audience that "we're all homosexual men," and then all the other drag queens—Sushi ("from Japan or somewhere"), Inga ("the Barbie girl of Sweden"), Kylie Jean Lucille ("the California dream"), Milla ("the Georgia peach"), Scabola Feces ("the pretty one, from Providence, Rhode Island, and Fire Island") and Margo ("the oldest living drag queen in captivity")—joined him on stage, dressed as men. (Well, Sushi, the only one not also introduced with his male name, tends to come out dressed only in tiny black bikini underpants with a red feather poof in front and a red boa, but he does have a bare chest.)

We were hooked. We came back again and again, let Milla perform with our little dog Emma, talked to the Bourbon Street Girls before and after their performances, told them that I was writing a history of same-sex love and sexuality and wanted to write about this show, even wangled an invitation to their drag queen meetings on Monday afternoons. ("That's when we get paid," Sushi told us, "so everyone shows up.") We're still hoping to get to a meeting and to understand this new kind of drag—maybe even to understand what makes a man a man and what makes a woman a woman.

The show illustrates for me both how much has changed and how much the past lives on in contemporary gay and lesbian worlds. I ask myself why I love drag so much, and I wonder if it is the playing with gender and sexuality, my own drag queen taste in fashion (I've taken to silver sparkle nail polish and a green chenille boa, and I've always loved lace and velvet), or my sense of connection with the long history of drag. For drag reminds me of eighteenth-century mollies who dressed in women's clothing, of Jeanne Bonnet shot dead in nineteenth-century San Francisco, of Harlem balls and fairies on street corners and Gladys Bentley in her white tux. Even as I also resist the notion that we are all "a people," because the meaning of sexual desires and acts has changed so dramatically over time.

In this last chapter, I do not try to tell a comprehensive story of contemporary gay and lesbian lives. Rather, I want to look at the ways that, from Stonewall on, new developments in the history of same-sex sexuality blend with continuities, creating a recent past, a present, and an imagined future that are neither completely novel nor simply more of the same.

Stonewall

On the night of June 27, 1969, the New York City police descended on the Stonewall Inn, a Greenwich Village gay bar, for what should have been a routine raid. But this night

R. V. Beaumont performing "What Makes a Man a Man?" April 1998, 801 Bar, Key West, Florida.

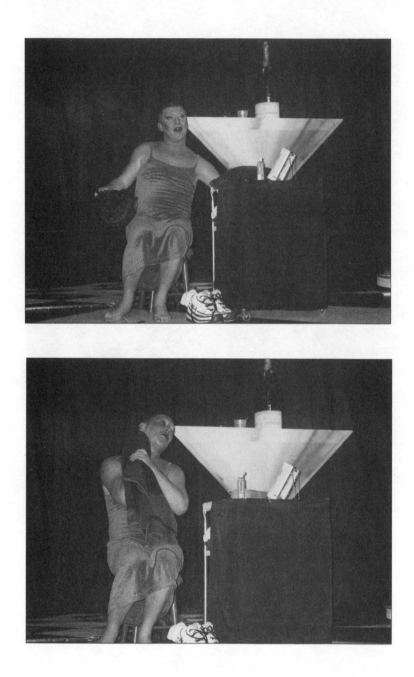

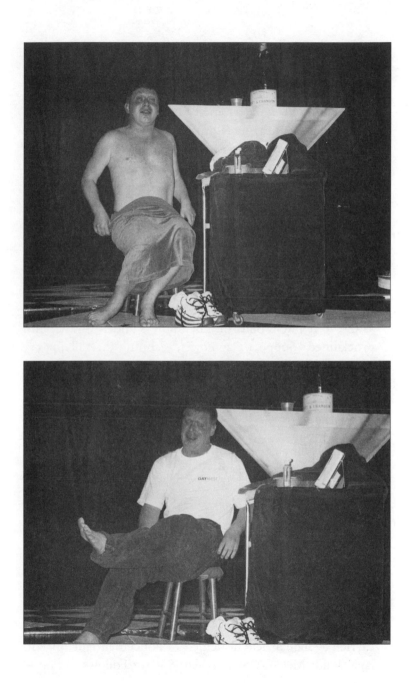

was special. Rather than submitting peacefully to arrest, the patrons—a young, racially mixed crowd of mostly men—fought back. Here is how the *Village Voice* described the scene:

Suddenly the paddywagon arrived and the mood of the crowd changed. Three of the more blatant queens—in full drag—were loaded inside, along with the bartender and doorman, to a chorus of catcalls and boos from the crowd. A cry went up to push the paddywagon over, but it drove away before anything could happen. With its exit, the action waned momentarily. The next person to come out was a dyke, and she put up a struggle—from car to door to car again. It was at that moment that the scene became explosive. Limp wrists were forgotten. Beer cans and bottles were heaved at windows, and a rain of coins descended on the cops.[1]

Even before the broken glass had been swept up it was clear, as the *Voice* put it, that "the liberation is under way." Graffiti proclaimed "Support Gay Power," echoing the rallying cry of the Black Power movement. At the same time, not all the action expressed a new style of politics. The police that night confronted a chorus line of drag queens belting out their theme song:

> We are the Stonewall girls
> We wear our hair in curls
> We wear no underwear
> We show our pubic hair . . .
> We wear our dungarees
> Above our nelly knees![2]

If Stonewall represented a new beginning, it would have been hard to tell that from the mainstream publicity. Other than the *Voice*, few papers gave the incident any attention. The *New York Times*, on page 33 of the June 29 edition, carried a small article headlined "4 Policemen Hurt in 'Village' Raid: Melee Near Sheridan Square Follows Action at

Bar." The *Washington Post,* the *Chicago Tribune,* and even the *San Francisco Examiner/Chronicle* remained mute.[3] Ironically, given the subsequent assumption that Stonewall represented something entirely new and unprecedented, the Homophile Action League of Philadelphia greeted the event as a dramatic "turning point" in the history of the homophile movement, and in 1970 the Fourth of July Annual Reminder was dropped in favor of a march in New York commemorating Stonewall.[4]

So was this the beginning of a dramatic new social movement? It is telling that two women who later joined the Furies, a radical feminist collective formed in 1971 that played a starring role in the emergence of lesbian feminism, remember hearing about Stonewall from across the Atlantic. Each had left the country, in part running away from the consequences of desire for women, and each came back with fresh hope because of Stonewall.[5]

The events in Greenwich Village came to symbolize self-acceptance, pride, and resistance, in contrast to the assimilationist tendencies of the homophile movement. Shortly after Stonewall, New York Mattachine called a meeting to try to reassert control and to plead for patience and politeness. But it was too late. Those tired of the old ways and unwilling to keep quiet walked out of the meeting. Out of that exodus the New York Gay Liberation Front was born. Seemingly overnight, Gay Liberation Fronts appeared in cities from Philadelphia to Chicago to Los Angeles and in university towns such as Austin, Texas, and Tallahassee, Florida. Demanding immediate and profound change in the system, gay liberationists adopted militant strategies and proudly asserted their right to define their own sexualities. By 1973, more than eight hundred groups could be counted around the country.[6] Symbolizing the conflict between old and new, the homophile organizers of the final Annual Reminder in Philadelphia in 1969 struggled to rule out both the wearing of drag, leather, and hippy styles and hand-holding by participants.[7]

What happened at the Stonewall Inn reflected butch resistance and drag queen humor as well as the growing militance of homophile activism and the impact of the civil rights movement, the New Left, and the women's movement. That night bridged old and new. In its aftermath gay and lesbian worlds changed in some dramatic ways but in other ways remained very much the same.

"Your Gloves Don't Match Your Shoes"

The years since 1969 have witnessed both phenomenal progress in organizing, community building, and consciousness raising and also vigorous and often successful efforts to resist the changes favored by the gay and lesbian movement. When the Stonewall riot erupted, there were about fifty lesbian or gay groups across the country, but by 1973 these had proliferated into more than a thousand. The National Gay Task Force, later renamed the National Gay and Lesbian Task Force, founded in 1973, originally brought together a mostly white, male, and middle-class membership interested in political action, and the Human Rights Campaign Fund, created in 1980, began to raise funds to support "gay friendly" candidates for political office. The National Coalition of Black Lesbians and Gays, dating to 1978, was the first national organization for African American gay men and lesbians.[8] Increasingly, as groups multiplied, they specialized in particular constituencies (lesbians, people of color, students, people of different religious affiliations, members of the military) or special purposes (politics, health, religion, sports). Big national marches in Washington in 1979 and 1987 brought together Jewish lesbians, black men in relationships with white men, transgendered people, South Asian queers, gay Mormons, People with AIDS—every imaginable identity (and some hardly imaginable) marching down the same streets. The AIDS crisis in particular mobilized gay men and lesbians and their supporters in an unprecedented fashion and gave rise to militant groups such as ACT-UP (AIDS Coalition to Unleash Power), founded in 1987, and Queer Nation, created in 1990. Lesbian Avengers, begun in New York in 1992, also embraced the new "in-your-face" style of action, proclaiming itself "loud, bold, sexy, silly, fierce, tasty and dramatic."[9]

The lesbian and gay movement fought for legal protection, winning a ruling in California in 1979 that "coming out" at work was an issue of free speech protected by the Constitution. In 1974 New York Democrats Bella Abzug and Ed Koch introduced in Congress the first federal civil rights bill for gay men and lesbians.[10] Yet this tactic came to naught. And although the fight to overturn the sodomy laws at the level of the Supreme Court suffered a severe blow with the 1986 *Bowers v. Hardwick* decision that upheld Georgia's sodomy law, more than thirty states (including Georgia in 1998) have decriminalized sodomy.[11]

The movement also sought to elect openly gay people to public office. Elaine Nobel won distinction as the first when she won, by a slim margin, a seat in the Massachusetts House of Representatives in 1974. In 1977 Harvey Milk, a businessman in the Castro district of San Francisco, received enough votes to serve on the city's Board of Supervisors. A year later, a disgruntled conservative colleague on the board killed Milk and Mayor George Moscone. When the murder case ended in a verdict of manslaughter, the gay community rose up in outrage, marching on city hall and eventually erupting in a riot of window smashing and arson.[12]

At the same time, as organizing proceeded apace, the gay and lesbian community spawned a wide variety of institutions

Maria and Tracy, New York Lesbian and Gay Pride March,
June 24, 1979. Copyright 1998 JEB (Joan E. Biren).

in addition to the traditional bars: restaurants, bookstores,
shops, business guilds, bowling leagues, substance abuse support groups, groups for "slightly older lesbians." Some of
these grew directly from the movement, but the commercial
marketplace also responded to the growth of a constituency
of gay and lesbian consumers, producing magazines, books,
films, and even credit cards that offer a percentage to movement organizations. Gay and lesbian neighborhoods—places
where houses flew the rainbow flag, designed in San Francisco
in 1978—sprang up across the country.[13] Some had long
histories, such as Greenwich Village; Cherry Grove and the
Pines on Fire Island, New York; Provincetown, Massachusetts;
and Key West, Florida. Others, such as West Hollywood,
California, Park Slope in Brooklyn, and even whole towns
such as Northhampton, Massachusetts, and Guerneville, California, developed gay or lesbian reputations. But even cities
without a history of residential same-sex clusters tend to
sport neighborhoods with such a reputation. My own city

of Columbus, Ohio, includes German Village, a gentrified area of brick Victorian houses and cobblestone streets close to downtown, home to many gay businesses and gay men. We live in a part of town called Clintonville, known jokingly as "Clitville" in some lesbian circles because of the many lesbians who live here.

The result of such growth, in organizations and community institutions, has been a transformation in gay and lesbian consciousness. The early homophile movement was formed in an atmosphere of public condemnation of homosexuality. Timid as they could be, the homophile groups began the process of countering the negative images of gay and lesbian people through their publications. But it was not until the 1970s that the gay and lesbian movement produced so many resources—newspapers, magazines, novels, self-help books, music, plays, films—that access to positive portrayals of gay and lesbian life had the potential to reach people in every corner of the country. Even representations not produced by the movement, such as television talk shows with their voyeuristic approach to gay, lesbian, bisexual, and transgendered people, have the capacity to reach millions of viewers, who listen despite themselves when the "freaks talk back."[14]

This is not to say that all people engaged in same-sex sexual activity, or even all people who identify as lesbian, gay, bisexual, or transgendered, support the movement in the late 1990s. But even for those who remain closeted or who disdain politics or who find the movement inhospitable, the world has undergone a sea change as a result of new forms of activism.

At the same time, the dual tendencies of earlier phases of organizing can be found in the contemporary movement. That is, there are still those who argue that the only difference between gay men and lesbians, on the one hand, and straight people, on the other, is the sex of those we desire, and that all we want is to be accepted as "normal" Americans. This impulse lies behind the drive to legalize same-sex marriage. In contrast, others embrace "queerness," insisting on our right to be as different as we like, to flout conventional sexual morality, styles of masculinity and femininity, and political mainstreaming.

In response to the movement's progress in organization, community building, and consciousness raising, the forces of opposition had changed by the 1980s. As the movement made strides toward repealing sodomy statutes in some (but not all) states, curtailing police harassment, removing homosexuality from the American Psychiatric Association's list of mental illnesses in 1974, challenging federal employment discrimination, and proposing civil rights legislation at the municipal and state levels, an organized and vocal counter-movement arose to challenge these gains. The New Right took on homosexuality as a major issue in the late 1970s, reviving all the traditional arguments about sin, sickness, and criminality. Organized groups fought against civil rights legislation, greeted the AIDS epidemic as just punishment from God, and called for the (sometimes literal) extermination of homosexuality from American society. Anita Bryant's Save Our Children organization succeeded in winning the repeal of a gay rights ordinance in Dade County, Florida, in 1977. This victory sparked other attempts to roll back the tide of the lesbian and gay movement. The election of Ronald Reagan to the presidency in 1980 marked a national shift to the political right. When the AIDS epidemic struck in 1981, first identified in the population of gay men, New Right groups such as Jerry Falwell's Moral Majority proclaimed the deadly disease God's revenge for immorality.[15]

So we can see how far we have come from the days of Jan Creoli's execution, yet how much we face the same timeworn arguments about "nature" and "God's laws." Henry Gerber might have been astonished by AIDS activists taunting the rubber-gloved police officers sent to arrest them with the chant, "Your gloves don't match your shoes," but the defiant drag queens arrested in Harlem would probably have joined right in.

A New World of Lesbian Feminism

When gay liberation burst onto the social movement scene in 1969, radical young activists pushed new ways of being gay. The "freaking fag revolutionary" who might sport a T-shirt proclaiming "Suck Cock to Beat the Draft" embraced gay sexuality along with a radical analysis that linked heterosexism to racism and capitalism.[16] But it was women rather than men who pioneered in establishing a new sexual and political identity, what became known as lesbian feminism.

The radical or "women's liberation" branch of the women's movement of the late 1960s and early 1970s gave birth to lesbian feminism. As women active in the civil rights and New Left movements began to apply a leftist analysis to their own situation as women and to chafe under the demeaning treatment they sometimes received from their male comrades, "radical feminists" began to argue that both capitalism and male supremacy oppressed women. Conceptualizing women as a "sex class," they increasingly called for separation from men—eventually even sexually.[17] Women who adopted the identity of "lesbian feminist" as a logical step in freeing themselves from male domination, but without having experienced sexual desire for a woman, saw lesbianism as a choice that any woman could make. These were the infamous "political lesbians" who so worried the Cincinnati lawyers. Yet there were also women who had long identified as lesbians who embraced lesbian feminism, especially since the mainstream women's movement was not particularly friendly to lesbians in the early 1970s. National

Organization for Women founder Betty Friedan, in an often-quoted dismissal, branded lesbianism the "lavender herring" of the women's movement, sparking a protest by lesbians at a women's movement conference in 1970.

Women within the Daughters of Bilitis had already begun to make connections between lesbianism and feminism when they distinguished their struggles from those of homosexual men and criticized the sexism of their male compatriots. Some women within the Gay Liberation Front went even further, attacking male sexuality as oppressive and fundamentally different from the female variety. Sexual difference was not, as we have seen, a new theme in Western culture. Even the Kinsey reports, which purported to show the essential similarity between male and female sexuality—tellingly labeled in the volume titles "human" sexuality—had ended up emphasizing different patterns of behavior and sexual response. But lesbian feminists reversed the values traditionally placed on male and female sexuality, revering female sexuality as diffuse, not goal oriented, fluid, and sensual and castigating male sexuality as narrow, rigid, and dominating. As one lesbian feminist put it in 1971: "Physicality is now a creative non-institutionalized experience. It is touching and rubbing and cuddling and fondness . . . . Its only goal is closeness and pleasure. It does not exist for the Big Orgasm. It exists for feeling nice. Our sexuality may or may not include genital experience."[18]

Not only did lesbian feminists redefine sex, but they also rejected butch/fem culture and defined "lesbian" as not necessarily having anything to do with sexuality. Anne Koedt, author of the enormously influential article "The Myth of the Vaginal Orgasm," proclaimed in 1972 that "role playing is sick."[19] Ti-Grace Atkinson, founder of the Radical Feminist October 17th Movement, also critiqued lesbian "role playing" as reinforcing the subordination of women. Early lesbian feminists saw themselves as gender outlaws, but in celebrating lack of conformity to traditional styles of masculinity and femininity they rejected both "dykes" and those women who desired dykes. Yet older styles of same-sex loving did not disappear with the advent of lesbian feminism. As one woman wrote in 1974 to a San Francisco publication, *Sisters*, "I'm still into [butch/fem life]. It feels right to me and that's what I consider to be where its at. I like me, I like being Gay, I like being Butch."[20] And bar lesbians in Albuquerque, New Mexico, voiced their own critique of lesbian feminists as unattractive and sloppy.[21]

Spurning old styles of loving women, lesbian feminists invented a new political definition, put most famously in the statement of Radicalesbians, an offshoot of the New York Gay Liberation Front: "What is a lesbian? A lesbian is the rage of all women condensed to the point of explosion."[22] This conception of lesbianism overturned all traditional notions by downplaying sexuality in favor of bonding between women and resistance to patriarchy. Lesbian feminists hoped to change the world by celebrating what they identified as the "female values" of egalitarianism, collectivism, caring, respect for knowledge derived from experience, pacifism, and cooperation; by building alternative institutions to allow women to live apart from men; and by politicizing everyday life through a rejection of femininity and consumerism. Lesbian feminists became identified as women who cut their hair short, didn't shave their armpits and legs, went without makeup, and wore comfortable, practical clothing such as flannel shirts, jeans, and boots.[23]

Because of this kind of self-presentation, because lesbian feminists played a critical role in the movement to combat rape and other forms of sexual violence against women, and because some women identified as lesbian feminists without any sexual desire for women, lesbian feminism has gained the reputation of being opposed to sexual passion. In the 1980s,

Pat, Lisa, and Moka, Michigan Womyn's Music Festival, 1977. The Music Festival is a central event in the lesbian feminist community. Copyright 1998 JEB (Joan E. Biren).

conflict around sexuality within the women's movement pitted those who emphasized the danger of sexuality (oppressive
heterosexuality, rape, childhood sexual abuse, domestic violence) against those who focused on the pleasure and rejected
the notion that some kinds of consensual sex are all right
and other kinds are bad. These "sex wars" identified lesbian
feminists as "antisex." Yet there were many women—both
those who already identified as lesbians and those who came
out in the context of the women's movement—for whom
lesbian feminism meant passionate and exciting sex. There
may have been an attempt to redefine what constituted sex,
there may have been a lesbian feminist "uniform," but that
doesn't mean (here it's time for me to claim my past) that we
didn't find each other sexy in those flannel shirts and jeans.
I don't deny that the hostility to butch/fem styles and the
rejection of anything that smacked of traditional femininity
alienated many women and contributed to the class and
ethnic exclusiveness of lesbian feminism. It did. But lesbian
feminism was not as sexless and humorless as critics would
have it. The Cincinnati lesbian feminist periodical *Dinah*, for
example, printed pleas for financial support full of sexual
innuendo and even explicit references to sex. "Put DINAH on
your chest," the editors urged readers in a 1978 sales pitch for
T-shirts. And *Dinah* contributors in 1977 could hope to win
"an authenticated Gertrude Stein orgasm. This 15 second tape
was discovered in 1963 in an attic in Paris and was certified
by Alice B. Toklas as an original."[24]

In fact both sides of the "sex wars" are part of the lesbian
feminist community.[25] Perhaps this is nowhere made clearer
than in the dueling titles of the main publications on opposite
sides of the battle lines. *Off Our Backs,* the classic radical
feminist newspaper, confronts *On Our Backs,* a magazine
with a sexual "bad girl" style. As a result of such clashes,
by the 1990s the lesbian feminist community saw the birth

of new kinds of identities or styles that built on butch/fem but played with both styles rather than adhering to a strict division. So we now we find butchy fems and femmy butches, soft butches and tomboy fems, lipstick lesbians and semibutch lesbian feminists, to use a collection of terms from recent personal ads.[26] Nothing could illustrate better the fluidity of the idea of what it means to be a lesbian.

The history of lesbian feminism shows how old and new identities merge and how much the way people view themselves can change over time. Conceptualizations of gender and sexuality have undergone revolutions within lesbian worlds from the 1950s to the 1970s to the 1990s. Yet in some ways we find that there is nothing new under the sun.

"It's Raining Men"

Perhaps just as revolutionary as women who explicitly linked their love and desire for women to a political critique of male dominance was the explosion among gay men of what became known as "clone culture" because of the uniform required "look." If the "dykes" of the new lesbian nation confused or alienated butches and fems by celebrating sexuality between two women who both rejected traditional femininity, the new and rapidly commercialized gay male culture might have had early twentieth-century fairies scratching their heads over the attraction between two "manly" men.

To go to the Castro, San Francisco's most celebrated gay male district, or to wander onto Christopher Street in New York in the 1970s and early 1980s was to believe that, as the famous Weathergirls song put it, "It's Raining Men."[27] And they all looked more or less alike: muscled body clad in a tight tank top (weather permitting), body-hugging Levi's 501 jeans, work boots, short hair, carefully trimmed mustache or beard. The music was disco, the sex was frequent and hot.

My friend Jack. Private collection, Columbus, Ohio.

In contrast to the middle- and upper-class men who had in the past sometimes cruised the streets of big cities looking for masculine working-class men to have sex with, clone culture itself embraced a working-class style. Instead of only desiring extreme masculinity, the men of this culture adopted it. They looked like incredibly well-groomed construction workers or cowboys or motorcycle gang members or soldiers or hoodlums or athletes or lumberjacks, but they made no attempt to appear straight. In this way they rejected the historical association between homosexuality and effeminacy.

At the same time, in other ways they behaved much the way men who desired men traditionally had. They frequented particular neighborhoods and institutions (gyms, bars, discos, bathhouses), they blatantly cruised each other on the streets, they adopted easily recognized uniforms, they spoke a special language of "circuits" and "cliques" and "tricks." But the meteoric growth of the gay community meant that now a man could live fully within this world. Young single urban men in the clone culture, most of them white and middle-class, had money to burn, and a commercial sector sprang up to cater to their tastes. As one twenty-seven-year-old New Yorker put it, "I live in an all-clone world. All my friends are clones. I live in a clone building, in a clone neighborhood, and work in a clone bar."[28]

Not all men, of course, lived a totally clone life. Just as women in the working-class butch/fem culture of the 1950s might change into butch dress to go the bar after work, so one New York man likened dressing as a clone to changing into play clothes as a child after coming home from school. "I come home from work, change into clone 'drag,' and go out and play on the circuit."[29] The "circuit" consisted of the "hot" spots—perhaps soon to fade into "tired"—that a particular crowd or clique favored. Hard partying and lots of drugs were part of the scene, especially on Saturday nights.

But the point of it all was sex, relatively anonymous sex and very "masculine" sex. The clone culture valued ruggedly handsome looks and large genitals. Men of color and working-class men (real ones) had a certain cachet, suggesting that the historical cross-class and cross-ethnic eroticism of male same-sex culture lingered. But physical attractiveness was the bottom line. "All that matters to me in a trick is how they look. They could be as dumb as shit or as boring as hell, but if they have a nice face, a big dick, or a good body, I'll fuck with them," as one man bluntly put it.[30] There was nothing subtle about cruising to find out the important things. As one man explained, "I'm a 'size queen.' Baskets often fool you. Asking someone if they have a big dick is too embarrassing. What I do instead is grope them."[31]

In a particularly striking exaggeration of traditional American masculine values, men of the clone culture not only objectified sex but separated it almost entirely from emotional intimacy. They had strong friendships, but not with the men they had sex with. "Sisters" were good friends, and "best friends" were like lovers except they didn't have sex with each other. "Tricks" were for casual and often anonymous sex; "fuck buddies" were for more regular sex but without any romantic involvement. Only "lovers" combined deep emotional and erotic connections, although often such a relationship did not exclude tricking with others. In a not atypical attack on monogamous lovers, one man described his disgust with "the kind that cling to each other and never trick with anyone else."[32]

Despite the embrace of masculinity, these were still gay men, eager to be noticed as gay men. First of all, they dressed immaculately, matching colors precisely, tailoring their clothes so they fit exactly right, and grooming themselves to perfection. If they aped construction workers, it was clear from the cleanliness of their clothes and hands that they didn't actually do physical labor. They wore costumes. When not publicly cruising they might lapse into more traditional ways of signifying their sexuality, such as referring to themselves with feminine pronouns. "Darling," one clone explained, "beneath all this butch drag, we are still girls."[33] Although men of the clone culture "dished," or gossiped about or criticized other men in a "bitchy" style, they masculinized this traditionally "camp" form by making it explicitly sexual:

"You tricked with her, the tooth fairy!" Tom snorted. "It's a good thing the Lord made her a dentist, because he certainly didn't give her a dick."

"I know," Sam chirped in. "She's so ashamed of its size that she doesn't shower or undress at the gym."[34]

Like lesbian feminists scorning butches and fems, men in the clone culture had little use for older-style gay men, even (or especially) though some of them had transformed themselves to fit the new styles. One man described men who "a couple of years ago . . . had puny bodies, lisping voices, and elegant clothes . . . . Now, they're 'butched up,' giving up limp wrists and mincing gaits for bulging muscles and manly handshakes."[35] When a group of cologned men in designer jeans and LaCoste shirts walked into a favorite New York clone bar, one man remarked, "Look at those trolls! . . . What are they doing here? Who let them in? . . . They're visual pollutants disrupting the erotic beauty of a room full of hot men."[36] Such attitudes remind us of the danger of assuming that all people with same-sex desire fit in the same conceptual category.

Much of this came to an end with the spread of AIDS through the clone community in the mid-1980s. Because of the frequency of the kinds of sex that proved so effective at transmitting HIV, this was the world ravaged by untimely death. Although the clone culture turned tragically deadly, it represents an important moment in time. Rejecting a necessary link between same-sex sexuality and gender inversion, gay clones claimed and refashioned masculinity. At the same time, that refashioning also drew on older ways of acknowledging and acting on same-sex desire.

Variety Is the Spice of Life

Although lesbian feminism and clone culture both can be characterized as dramatically new developments in the history of same-sex sexuality, the women and men who embraced these identities made up only a tiny proportion of those with same-sex desires. Gay and lesbian worlds since the 1960s have continued to encompass a whole range of people whose desires and behaviors and identities either are more similar to those of the past or are new but strikingly different from those pioneered in the 1970s and 1980s.

All over the country, for example, there are people who just live their lives with partners of the same sex but see themselves as no different (except for this one thing) from their neighbors. Some gay men and lesbians get married and raise families: they adopt children or raise children born in their own heterosexual relationships, or lesbians make use of artificial insemination to give birth to children. Some women identify as lesbians but claim the label "romantic friends."[37] Other women couples still live in what would have been called Boston marriages without considering themselves lesbians at all. Some men live their lives as, and claim the identity of, drag queens. (And now we have "drag kings" as well.) Two-Spirit People in some Native American communities still cross the lines of gender.[38] Women still deeply identify as butches and fems and organize their erotic and social lives around that dynamic.[39]

And in addition to people who proudly claim the identity "transgendered," there are those who still secretly cross the gender boundary. When jazz musician Billy Tipton died in 1989, the world (to say nothing of his wives and adopted sons) were astonished to learn that he was a woman. Although he originally invented himself as a man in order to earn a living during the depression, he embraced manhood in his later years in ways that suggest there was much more to it.[40]

Diverse groups within American society continue to adhere to their own ideas about sexuality and gender. In Latino communities, the Latin American sexual system that gives priority to the part a man plays in a sexual act rather than to the sex of his partner means that men can still engage in sex with other men, as long as they take the penis-wielding role, and not consider themselves, or be considered, gay.[41] At the same time, Chicana lesbian writer Cherríe Moraga relates her butch lesbian identity to the intense subordination of women in Mexican American communities (part of a pattern of resistance to Anglo oppression based on fierce loyalty to the family), suggesting why women of color have been forthright in criticizing lesbian feminist attacks on butch/fem ways of loving.[42] Differences between the ways that minority communities and the dominant culture perceive sexuality help to explain why Afro-Caribbean lesbian Makeda Silvera reports that her grandmother told her that loving women was "a white people ting" and Chinese American Eric C. Wat writes of the assumption in diverse Asian communities that homosexuality is a "white disease."[43] Yet minority communities also include tight social networks of gay men and lesbians. The African American expressions "one of the children" and "family" express the importance of friendships modeled on kinship for survival as a gay person of color.[44]

New identities and ways of conceiving of same-sex sexuality emerge all the time. As we have seen, young lesbians embrace styles that would have been anathema to the lesbian feminists of the 1970s. The "dyke punk" band Tribe 8 features two hard-core butch members, a sexy fem with low-cut shirt, and a lead singer who performs bare breasted with a dildo hanging out of her pants that she cuts off and flings into the audience.[45] Men who claim the identity of "bears" reject what they call the "twinks" style and celebrate a masculinity that is worlds apart from that of the clone culture.[46]

In other words, the concept of sexual identity has, in the mainstream of American society, come to refer to sexual-object choice, but there is no unanimity among the multiple class and ethnic and identity communities that make up American society as to what defines a man as gay or a woman as lesbian.

In looking to the future, we must acknowledge that schol-ars and activists today are working to question the very cate-gories "gay/lesbian," "heterosexual," and "bisexual." The term "queer," once embraced both by the fairies of Newport and by New York men with same-sex desires who rejected the fairy role, has now come to encompass all sorts of people who want to break out of categories and identities and take up fluid and unlimited sexualities. "Queer straights" may be married women who identify as gay men. Individuals born with male bodies who desire women may present a female gender and identify as lesbians. If some of this boggles the late twentieth-century mind, we would do well to remember the wide variety of understandings of sexuality in the past.

A Desired Past

The stories that have unfolded in *A Desired Past* show how complex the history of same-sex sexuality is. In fact, the individuals and groups we have encountered in these pages might be considered to fall into three broad and overlapping categories. Some experienced love or sexual desire, or both, for someone of the same sex. Others engaged in same-sex sexual acts. Still others crossed the lines of gender in some way, sometimes completely and sometimes partially. And of course some did two or three of these things.

We have seen that, although there have always been people who express desire for sexual contact with others of the same sex, there has not always been a meaning or an identity attached to such desires. The society constructed by European colonists disapproved of same-sex sexual conduct but did not entirely single it out from other nonmarital and nonprocreative sexual acts. Some Native American cultures, and some African cultures, developed social roles that included the possibility of same-sex sexuality, although gender transformation and spirituality, rather than sexuality, generally lay at the heart of those gender crossings.

Identity based on same-sex sexuality emerged in the United States in the course of the nineteenth century, although such identity was sometimes, at least for men, focused on gender inversion and sexual role rather than on sexual-object choice. Over time, "sodomites," "queers," "fairies," and "bulldaggers" became "homosexuals," "gay men," and "lesbians" as individuals not only claimed labels for themselves but began to gather with others like them and to assert their right to live and love openly. Cultures ranged from those emerging out of sex segregation (on the frontier, in boarding schools, and yes, Dad, in women's colleges) to intentional ones growing up in urban areas around institutions such as taverns, brothels, bars, and lodging places. Same-sex cultures, in turn, formed the foundation of the social movement that sprang up in the 1950s. That movement has helped to define further gay and lesbian identities—and increasingly, as well, bisexual and transgendered identities—that emphasize the significance of sexual desire and gender presentation not just for love and passion but for all aspects of human life.

Lest, however, we see this as the triumphal end of the story and view everything that has gone before as inexorably culminating in the present, I want to emphasize again the multiple and changing meanings of sexual desire and behavior that we see in both the past and the present.

I have had a recurring dream since childhood. I'm in my house, although it isn't always where I actually live, and I find a door that opens into a whole part of the house I've never known about. Sometimes it's an attic, sometimes it's an entire wing. Sometimes there are sun porches and tower rooms and gables—things I crave in houses. It's all usually dusty and in disrepair. I marvel that all this has been hidden away, just behind a door I'd never opened. It's a really good dream.

I never thought much about what it meant, maybe because I know almost nothing about dream analysis. But when I was thinking about the conclusion to this book, the dream popped into my head. I guess because I'm a card-carrying historian rather than a psychoanalyst, I don't think the dream is about unexplored aspects of my sexuality. Rather, I think it's about discovering new things about the past.

So now I have a fantasy that I find the secret rooms and in them are the people I've written about here. In one version of this fantasy (the version I resist), everyone mingles and chats as if they are at a cocktail party. Horatio Alger and a fairy from the 1920s compare notes about New York, while mid-nineteenth-century romantic friends Molly and Helena reassure Chinese American physician Margaret Chung that she is normal. In my more likely version of this fantasy, almost everyone is staring incredulously at everyone else. Perhaps, at most, Nicholas Sension, the seventeenth-century Connecticut man who pursued his servant boys, thinks he might have something in common with Walt Whitman, and Jeanne Bonnet, the cross-dressing San Francisco gang leader who was murdered in 1876, stares with admiration at a group of 1950s butches. But mostly everyone mills around wondering what all these strange people are doing there.

But my favorite part of the fantasy is this: Aunt Leila walks over to me. She looks around disdainfully and says, "Who *are* all these people, Leila Jane?" (She was "Leila Henrietta," although she'd have killed me for writing that.) And then she says, "What I wanted to tell you is that I loved Diantha the way you love Verta."

And the best part of this is that, even though this is my fantasy, I'm still not sure what she means.

Notes

Chapter One

1. Huussen 1989, 146.
2. Cook 1992, 479, 15.
3. Freedman 1998; see also Freedman 1996.
4. Duberman 1989.
5. Vance 1989 raises this last question, attributing it to one of her students, in an extremely thoughtful article. On New Guinea, see Herdt 1981.
6. Katz 1995, 20. Katz cites Dr. James G. Kiernan, "Responsibility in Sexual Perversion," *Chicago Medical Recorder* 3 (May 1892): 185–210.
7. This is the historical position known as "essentialism," most closely associated with the late John Boswell. See Boswell 1980, 1994. His theoretical position is perhaps best laid out in Boswell 1989. Another historical work emphasizing similarities rather than differences across time is Norton 1992. It is important to emphasize here that the issue for historians is less the biological or social *origin* of same-sex desire than the similarity of its manifestations in different cultures.
8. Most historians of sexuality are "social constructionists," that is, they focus on understanding the ways social forces have shaped sexuality differently in different cultures. Stein 1990 collects many of the classic articles on social constructionism.
9. See Halperin 1989; Padgug 1989.
10. Lister 1988, 1992.

Chapter Two

1. Trexler 1995.
2. Feinberg 1996.
3. Sams 1916, 80–81.
4. Gutiérrez 1991, 12, 19.
5. Delâge 1993, 57–59, 201–4.
6. Sams 1916, 65.
7. Quoted in Katz 1976, 289.
8. Greenberg 1988.
9. See Williams 1986; Allen 1986; Jacobs, Thomas, and Lang 1997.

10. Quoted in Katz 1976, 290.

11. Quoted in Katz 1976, 287.

12. Quoted in Katz 1976, 285–90.

13. Quoted in Greenberg 1988, 40–41.

14. Quoted in Gutiérrez 1991, 35.

15. Quoted in Saslow 1989, 92.

16. Quoted in Trumbach 1989, 131.

17. Burg 1984, 147, 146. See also, for a slightly later period, Gilbert 1976.

18. Quoted in Rey 1985, 181.

19. Quoted in Trumbach 1989, 137.

20. Quoted in Brown 1989.

21. Quoted in Faderman 1981, 51.

22. Faderman 1981, 51–52. As suggested by Joanne Meyerowitz, I follow here the practice of the transgender movement in using pronouns according to the gender of presentation.

23. Quoted in Faderman 1981, 57. "Randy women" is a rough translation of *lollepotten,* a term analyzed in Everard 1994.

24. See Bleys 1995, 33.

25. Quoted in Bleys 1995, 33.

26. Bleys 1995, 33.

27. Quoted in Baum 1993, 25. All information in this paragraph is from Baum.

28. Katz 1976, 22–23.

29. Bleys 1995, 34.

30. Bleys 1995, 34.

31. Quoted in Bleys 1995, 34.

32. Bleys 1995, 34.

33. Quoted in Katz 1976, 19–20.

34. Quoted in Katz 1983, 94–100.

35. Quoted in Katz 1983, 85–86, 92–93.

36. Godbeer 1995, 266–67.

37. Katz 1983, 68.

38. Quoted in Godbeer 1995, 263.

39. All quotations in this and the similar cases come from Godbeer 1995.

40. This discussion is based on Brown 1995 and Norton 1997.

41. Quoted in Norton 1997, 42.

42. Quoted in Brown 1995, 182.

43. Quoted in Brown 1995, 183.

44. Norton 1997, 41.

45. Quoted in Norton 1997, 44.

46. This is the fascinating interpretation developed by Norton 1997, 59.

Chapter Three

1. Smith-Rosenberg 1975.

2. Quoted in Smith-Rosenberg 1975, 5–7.

3. Quoted in an e-mail communication from John Weiss, 2 April 1998; Weiss found this reference in the course of his research on African Americans who took their freedom in the course of the War of 1812. I am grateful for his permission to cite this document. See Weiss 1996.

4. Quoted in Smith-Rosenberg 1975, 4–5.

5. Quoted in D'Emilio and Freedman 1988, 126.

6. Quoted in Smith-Rosenberg 1975, 24–26.

7. See Holloway 1997.

8. Quoted in Knowlton 1997, 45.

9. Quoted in Knowlton 1997, 48.

10. Quoted in Rotundo 1989, 7.

11. Quoted in Rotundo 1989, 4.

12. D'Emilio and Freedman 1988, 127.

13. Quoted in Katz 1976, 472–73.

14. See Donald 1995 and Chauncey 1998.

15. Quoted in Duberman 1991, 63.

16. Quoted in Duberman 1989, 155.

17. Quoted in Hansen 1995, 159, 160.

18. Quoted in Hansen 1995, 160.

19. Quoted in Hansen 1995, 162.

20. Quoted in Hansen 1995, 164.

21. Quoted in Hansen 1995, 168.

22. Quoted in Hansen 1995, 170.

23. Both quoted in Smith-Rosenberg 1985, 106.

24. Allmendinger 1992, 6. Allmendinger sees this as symbolic of the cowboys' own "castration" in being isolated from women; I see it, rather, as potentially homoerotic.

25. Clarence Ulford, *Tex* (New York: Burt, 1922), 212; quoted in Katz 1976, 510.

26. Quoted in Williams 1986, 158.

27. Quoted in Perry 1997, 516.

28. Quoted in Williams 1986, 159.

29. Williams 1986, 159–60.

30. Quoted in Westermeier 1974, 101.

31. Ng 1989; Hinsch 1990.

32. Friday 1994, 54–55, 114; Mason and Guimary 1981. I am grateful to Judy Tzu-Chun Wu for these references.

33. Quoted in Quinn 1996, 113.

34. Quinn 1996, 233–42.

35. Quinn 1996, 233, 242–44.

36. Goldman 1981.

37. San Francisco Lesbian and Gay History Project 1989.

38. On the historical associations between prostitution and lesbianism, see Nestle 1987.

39. Quoted in Miller 1997, 8.

40. Quoted in Miller 1997, 11.

41. Quoted in San Francisco Lesbian and Gay History Project 1989, 188.

42. Nestle 1987, 239.

43. Quoted in San Francisco Lesbian and Gay History Project 1989, 187.

44. Katz 1976, 509–10.

45. Quoted in Westermeier 1974, 104.

46. Quoted in Katz 1976, 293–98.

47. Quoted in Katz 1976, 304–8.

48. Quoted in Katz 1976, 299.

49. Quoted in Katz 1976, 300.

50. Quoted in Katz 1976, 313–17; see also Roscoe 1988.

51. Quoted in Katz 1976, 301.

52. Quoted in Williams 1986, 172–73.

53. Quoted in Williams 1986, 179.

54. Williams 1986, 180.

55. Quoted in Moon 1987, 91.

56. Quoted in Moon 1987, 94.

57. Quoted in Gorn 1986, 74.

58. Quoted in Shively 1987, 11–12.

59. Quoted in Shively 1987, 19.

60. Quoted in Shively 1987, 52.

61. Quoted in Katz 1976, 338–39.

62. Quoted in Shively 1987, 67.

63. Quoted in Shively 1987, 100.

64. Quoted in Reynolds 1995, 250.

65. Quoted in Burnham 1973, 41.

Chapter Four

1. Duggan 1994.

2. Quoted in Katz 1983, 157.

3. Quoted in Burnham 1973, 41.
4. Quoted in Burnham 1973, 46.
5. Quoted in Mumford 1996, 399.
6. Quoted in Katz 1983, 218–22.
7. Quoted in Chauncey 1982–83, 119.
8. Quoted in Chauncey 1982–83, 118.
9. Quoted in Katz 1995, 20.
10. Quoted in Smith-Rosenberg 1989, 269.
11. Quoted in Chauncey 1982–83, 120.
12. Quoted in Chauncey 1982–83, 122.
13. Quoted in Chauncey 1982–83, 123.
14. Quoted in Chauncey 1982–83, 129.
15. Quoted in Taylor 1980, 225.
16. Quoted in Terry 1991, 67.
17. Quoted in Chauncey 1982–83, 138.
18. Quoted in Reynolds 1995, 198.
19. The evidence is discussed in detail in Reynolds 1995, 70–80.
20. Shively 1987, 23–24.
21. See Lunbeck 1994, 297.
22. Quoted in Sahli 1979, 21.
23. Quoted in Faderman 1991, 35.
24. Quoted in Hull 1987, 139.
25. Quoted in Faderman 1991, 52.
26. Rupp 1997, 581.
27. Cook 1977.
28. Quoted in Faderman 1991, 26.
29. Quoted in Rupp 1997, 583–84.
30. Quoted in Rupp 1997, 584–85.
31. Horowitz 1994.
32. Quoted in Faderman 1991, 53.
33. Quoted in Faderman 1991, 54.
34. Freedman 1996.
35. Quoted in Smith-Rosenberg 1989, 275.
36. See Duggan 1993.
37. Quoted in Ullman 1995, 593.
38. Quoted in Ullman 1995, 594.
39. Quoted in Ullman 1995, 595.
40. See Chauncey 1989.
41. Quoted in Ullman 1995, 597.
42. Quoted in Chauncey 1989, 299.
43. Quoted in Chauncey 1989, 306.
44. Quoted in Chauncey 1989, 308.

45. Quoted in Chauncey 1995, 310.
46. Quoted in Chauncey 1995, 314.
47. Russell 1993, 33.
48. Quoted in History Project 1998, 103.

Chapter Five
1. See Chauncey 1994, 14–18, and Nestle 1993.
2. Quoted in Katz 1983, 329.
3. Quoted in Johnson 1997, 98.
4. Quoted in Johnson 1997, 104.
5. Quoted in Johnson 1997, 102.
6. Quoted in Chauncey 1994, 42.
7. Quoted in Chauncey 1994, 237.
8. Quoted in Mumford 1996, 404.
9. Quoted in Katz 1983, 447.
10. Quoted in Garber 1989, 320.
11. Nestle 1993, 932–33.
12. Quoted in Chauncey 1994, 248.
13. Quoted in Meyerowitz 1988, 114.
14. Johnson 1997, 104.
15. Boyd 1997.
16. Quoted in Chauncey 1989, 298.
17. Quoted in Drexel 1997, 126.
18. Quoted in Johnson 1993, 5.
19. Quoted in Chauncey 1989, 300.
20. Johnson 1997, 97.
21. Chauncey 1994, 52.
22. Quoted in Johnson 1993, 14.
23. Quoted in Johnson 1993, 19.
24. Chauncey 1994, 58.
25. Quoted in White 1993, 93.
26. Quoted in White 1993, 95.
27. Quoted in Chauncey 1994, 66.
28. Quoted in Drexel 1997, 125.
29. Chauncey 1994.
30. Chauncey 1994.
31. Quoted in Chauncey 1994, 103.
32. Quoted in Howard 1997a, 3.
33. Quoted in History Project 1998, 124.
34. Quoted in Chauncey 1994, 109.
35. Quoted in Ullman 1995, 578.
36. Quoted in Ullman 1995, 590.

37. Quoted in Chauncey 1994, 257.
38. Quoted in Katz 1983, 453.
39. Quoted in History Project 1998, 105.
40. Quoted in Katz 1976, 83, 90.
41. Boyd 1997.
42. Chauncey 1994.
43. Bullough and Bullough 1977.
44. Quoted in Bullough and Bullough 1977, 897.
45. Quoted in Bullough and Bullough 1977, 902.
46. Kennedy 1996.
47. Kennedy 1996, 26.
48. Quoted in Kennedy 1996, 27.
49. Quoted in Kennedy 1996, 31.
50. Quoted in Katz 1983, 305.
51. Quoted in Katz 1983, 396–97.
52. Russell 1993, 100.

Chapter Six
1. Quoted in Bérubé 1990, 31.
2. Quoted in Bérubé 1990, 17.
3. Quoted in Bérubé 1990, 8.
4. Quoted in Bérubé 1990, 32.
5. Quoted in Meyer 1996, 157.
6. Meyer 1996.
7. Quoted in Bérubé 1990, 43.
8. Quoted in Meyer 1996, 166.
9. Quoted in Bérubé 1990, 50.
10. Bérubé 1990.
11. Bérubé 1990.
12. Quoted in Bérubé 1990, 137.
13. Quoted in Bérubé 1990, 206–7.
14. Quoted in Bérubé 1990, 232.
15. Quoted in D'Emilio 1983, 46.
16. Quoted in D'Emilio 1983, 42.
17. Quoted in D'Emilio 1992, 60.
18. Quoted in Freedman 1987, 94.
19. D'Emilio 1983, 50.
20. See D'Emilio 1992.
21. D'Emilio 1983, 48.
22. Quoted in Bérubé 1990, 233.
23. Quoted in Bérubé 1990, 237.
24. Quoted in Bérubé 1990, 252.

25. Kinsey, Pomeroy, and Martin 1948; Kinsey et al. 1953; see Stein 1994, 94–95.

26. Bannon 1983, 1.

27. Russo 1987.

28. Quoted in D'Emilio 1983, 179.

29. Quoted in Stein 1994, 181.

30. Quoted in Drexel 1997, 136.

31. Quoted in Newton 1993, 39.

32. Quoted in Newton 1993, 67.

33. Quoted in Boyd 1997, 73.

34. Quoted in Beemyn 1997, 195.

35. Quoted in Retzloff 1997, 227–28.

36. Retzloff 1997.

37. Howard 1997b.

38. Franzen 1993.

39. Buring 1997.

40. Stein 1998; Thorpe 1997.

41. Quoted in Kennedy and Davis 1993, 76. The entire discussion is heavily indebted to Kennedy and Davis.

42. Quoted in Faderman 1991, 159.

43. Quoted in Kennedy and Davis 1993, 179.

44. Quoted in Kennedy and Davis 1993, 191.

45. Nestle 1984, 233.

46. Quoted in Kennedy and Davis 1993, 107.

47. Quoted in Thorpe 1997, 166.

48. Quoted in Kennedy and Davis 1993, 355.

49. Nestle 1981.

50. Cook 1992.

51. Orleck 1995.

52. Quoted in Orleck 1995, 137.

53. Quoted in Orleck 1995, 282.

54. Quoted in Orleck 1995, 283; see also 310.

55. Wu 1997.

56. Wu 1997, 22.

57. Quoted in Wu 1997, 24.

58. Quoted in Wu 1997, 33.

59. Quoted in Wu 1997, 25.

60. Quoted in Wu 1997, 26.

61. Quoted in Wu 1997, 30–31.

62. Quoted in Chauncey 1994, 249.

63. Quoted in Katz 1976, 387.

64. Quoted in Haeberle 1984, 130.

65. D'Emilio 1983. This discussion of the homophile movement is indebted to D'Emilio.

66. Quoted in D'Emilio 1983, 81.

67. Quoted in D'Emilio 1983, 115.

68. Quoted in Faderman 1991, 180.

69. Quoted in Kennedy and Davis 1993, 187.

70. Quoted in Faderman 1991, 163.

71. Freeman, n.d.

72. Quoted in D'Emilio 1983, 158.

73. Quoted in Stein 1994, 218.

74. Quoted in Stein 1994, 210.

75. Stein, n.d.

76. This discussion is based on D'Emilio 1995.

77. Quoted in D'Emilio 1995, 88.

78. Quoted in Stein 1994, 338.

79. Weiss and Schiller 1988, 62, 60.

80. Stein, n.d.

81. D'Emilio 1983, 227.

82. On the campaign against the Walt Whitman bridge, see Stein 1994.

Chapter Seven

1. Truscott 1969.

2. Quoted in Duberman 1993, 201.

3. Moum 1992.

4. Stein, n.d.

5. Personal communication, the Furies' twenty-fifth reunion, Oxford, Ohio, April 1996.

6. Duberman 1993.

7. Stein, 1999.

8. See Epstein, 1999.

9. Quoted in Taylor and Rupp 1993, 53.

10. See Epstein, 1999.

11. Bernstein 1998.

12. Epstein, 1999.

13. Epstein, 1999.

14. Gamson 1998.

15. Epstein, 1999.

16. Kissack 1995, 109.

17. See Taylor and Rupp 1993.

18. Quoted in Echols 1989, 218.

19. Quoted in Cofield 1996, 11.

20. Quoted in Cofield 1996, 39.

21. Franzen 1993.

22. Radicalesbians, "The Woman Identified Woman," in Koedt, Levine, and Rapone 1973, 240.

23. See Taylor and Rupp 1993.

24. Quoted in Freeman, n.d.

25. See Taylor and Rupp 1993.

26. These terms come from ads in *On Our Backs* and the *Gay Community News;* cited in Cofield 1996, 55–56.

27. This is the title Michael Kimmel chose for a chapter of Levine 1998, on which this discussion is based.

28. Quoted in Levine 1998, 30.

29. Quoted in Levine 1998, 59.

30. Quoted in Levine 1998, 93.

31. Quoted in Levine 1998, 87.

32. Quoted in Levine 1998, 108.

33. Quoted in Levine 1998, 63.

34. Quoted in Levine 1998, 72.

35. Quoted in Levine 1998, 55.

36. Quoted in Levine 1998, 51.

37. Rothblum and Brehony 1993.

38. Williams 1986; Allen 1989.

39. Nestle 1992.

40. See Middlebrook 1998.

41. See Almaguer 1991.

42. See Moraga 1983 and Moraga and Hollibaugh 1983.

43. Silvera 1992, 523; Wat 1996, 76.

44. Hawkeswood 1997.

45. See Alfonso and Trigilio 1997.

46. Wright 1997.

References

Alfonso, Rita, and Jo Trigilio. 1997. "Surfing the Third Wave: A Dialogue between Two Third Wave Feminists." *Hypatia* 12, no. 3:7–15.

Allen, Paula Gunn. 1986. *The Sacred Hoop*. Boston: Beacon Press.

———. 1989. "Lesbians in American Indian Cultures." In *Hidden from History: Reclaiming the Gay and Lesbian Past*, edited by Martin Bauml Duberman, Martha Vicinus, and George Chauncey Jr., 106–17. New York: New American Library.

Allmendinger, Blake. 1992. *The Cowboy: Representations of Labor in an American Work Culture*. New York: Oxford University Press.

Almaguer, Tomás. 1991. "Chicano Men: A Cartography of Homosexual Identity and Behavior." *Differences: A Journal of Feminist Cultural Studies* 3, no. 2:75–100.

Bannon, Ann. [1957] 1983. *Odd Girl Out*. Tallahassee, Fla: Volute Books.

Baum, Robert M. 1993. "Homosexuality and the Traditional Religions of the Americas and Africa." In *Homosexuality and World Religions*, edited by Arlene Swidler, 1–46. Valley Forge, Pa.: Trinity Press International.

Beemyn, Brett. 1997. "A Queer Capital: Race, Class, Gender, and the Changing Social Landscape of Washington's Gay Communities, 1940–1955." In *Creating a Place for Ourselves: Lesbian, Gay, and Bisexual Community Histories*, edited by Brett Beemyn, 183–209. New York: Routledge.

Bernstein, Mary. 1998. "Social Movement Activism and Legal Change: The Lesbian and Gay Movement and the Decriminalization of Sodomy." Paper presented at the meetings of the American Sociological Association, San Francisco.

Bérubé, Allan. 1990. *Coming out under Fire: The History of Gay Men and Women in World War II*. New York: Free Press.

Bleys, Rudi C. 1995. *The Geography of Perversion: Male-to-Male Sexual Behavior outside the West and the Ethnographic Imagination, 1750–1918*. New York: New York University Press.

Boswell, John. 1980. *Christianity, Social Tolerance, and Homosexuality: Gay People in Western Europe from the Beginning of the*

Christian Era to the Fourteenth Century. Chicago: University of Chicago Press.

———. 1989. "Revolutions, Universals, and Sexual Categories." In *Hidden from History: Reclaiming the Gay and Lesbian Past,* edited by Martin Bauml Duberman, Martha Vicinus, and George Chauncey Jr., 17–36. New York: New American Library.

———. 1994. *Same-Sex Unions in Premodern Europe.* New York: Villard.

Boyd, Nan Alamilla. 1997. " 'Homos Invade S.F.!' San Francisco's History as a Wide-Open Town." In *Creating a Place for Ourselves: Lesbian, Gay, and Bisexual Community Histories,* edited by Brett Beemyn, 73–95. New York: Routledge.

Brown, Judith C. 1989. "Lesbian Sexuality in Medieval and Early Modern Europe." In *Hidden from History: Reclaiming the Gay and Lesbian Past,* edited by Martin Bauml Duberman, Martha Vicinus, and George Chauncey Jr., 67–75. New York: New American Library.

Brown, Kathleen. 1995. " 'Changed . . . into the Fashion of Man': The Politics of Sexual Difference in a Seventeenth-Century Anglo-American Settlement." *Journal of the History of Sexuality* 6:171–93.

Bullough, Vern, and Bonnie Bullough. 1977. "Lesbianism in the 1920s and 1930s: A Newfound Study." *Signs: Journal of Women in Culture and Society* 2, no. 4:895–904.

Burg, B. R. 1984. *Sodomy and the Pirate Tradition: English Sea Rovers in the Seventeenth-Century Caribbean.* New York: New York University Press.

Buring, Daneel. 1997. "Softball and Alcohol: The Limits of Lesbian Community in Memphis from the 1940s through the 1960s." In *Carryin' on in the Lesbian and Gay South,* edited by John Howard, 203–23. New York: New York University Press.

Burnham, John. 1973. "Early References to Homosexual Communities in American Medical Writings." *Medical Aspects of Human Sexuality* 7 (August): 34–49.

Chauncey, George, Jr. 1982–83. "From Sexual Inversion to Homosexuality: Medicine and the Changing Conceptualization of Female Deviance." *Salmagundi* 58–59 (fall–winter): 114–46.

———. 1989. "Christian Brotherhood or Sexual Perversion? Homosexual Identities and the Construction of Sexual Boundaries in the World War I Era." In *Hidden from History: Reclaiming the Gay and Lesbian Past,* edited by Martin Bauml Duberman, Martha Vicinus, and George Chauncey Jr., 294–317. New York: New American Library.

————. 1994. *Gay New York: Gender, Urban Culture, and the Making of the Gay Male World, 1890–1940.* New York: Basic Books.

————. 1998. "The Ridicule of Gay and Lesbian Studies Threatens All Academic Inquiry." *Chronicle of Higher Education* 44, no. 43:A40.

Cofield, Alexis A. 1996. "Butch and Fem to Butchy-Femme and Femmy-Butch: The Impact of Lesbian Feminism on the Construction of Butch and Fem Identities from the 1970s to the Present." M.A. thesis, Ohio State University.

Cook, Blanche Wiesen. 1977. "Female Support Networks and Political Activism." *Chrysalis* 3 (autumn): 43–61.

————. 1992. *Eleanor Roosevelt.* Vol. 1. *1884–1933.* New York: Viking.

Delâge, Denys. 1993. *Bitter Feast: Amerindians and Europeans in North-eastern North America, 1600–64.* Translated by Jane Brierly. Vancouver: University of British Columbia Press.

D'Emilio, John. 1983. *Sexual Politics, Sexual Communities: The Making of a Homosexual Minority in the United States, 1940–1970.* Chicago: University of Chicago Press.

————. 1992. *Making Trouble: Essays on Gay History, Politics, and the University.* New York: Routledge.

————. 1995. "Homophobia and the Trajectory of Postwar American Radicalism: The Career of Bayard Rustin." *Radical History Review* 62 (spring): 80–103.

D'Emilio, John, and Estelle B. Freedman. 1988. *Intimate Matters: A History of Sexuality in America.* New York: Harper and Row.

Donald, David Herbert. 1995. *Lincoln.* New York: Simon and Schuster.

Drexel, Allen. 1997. "Before Paris Burned: Race, Class, and Male Homosexuality on the Chicago South Side, 1935–1960." In *Creating a Place for Ourselves: Lesbian, Gay, and Bisexual Communities,* edited by Brett Beemyn, 119–44. New York: Routledge.

Duberman, Martin Bauml. 1989. " 'Writhing Bedfellows' in Antebellum South Carolina." In *Hidden from History: Reclaiming the Gay and Lesbian Past,* edited by Martin Bauml Duberman, Martha Vicinus, and George Chauncey Jr., 153–68. New York: New American Library.

————. 1991. *About Time: Exploring the Gay Past.* Rev. ed. New York: Meridian Books.

————. 1993. *Stonewall.* New York: Dutton.

Duggan, Lisa. 1993. "The Trials of Alice Mitchell: Sensationalism, Sexology, and the Lesbian Subject in Turn-of-the-Century America." *Signs:Journal of Women in Culture and Society* 18, no. 4:791–814.

————. 1994. "Queering the State." *Social Text,* no.38:1–14.

Echols, Alice. 1989. *Daring to Be Bad: Radical Feminism in America, 1967–1975.* Minneapolis: University of Minnesota Press.

Epstein, Steven. 1999. "Gay and Lesbian Movements in the United States: Dilemmas of Identity, Diversity, and Political Strategy." In *The Global Emergence of Gay and Lesbian Politics: National Imprints of a Worldwide Movement,* edited by Barry D. Adam, Jan Willem Duyvendak, and André Krouwel, 30–90. Philadelphia: Temple University Press.

Everard, Myriam Hermine Mathilde. 1994. "Ziel en zinnen: Over liefde en lust tussen vrouwen in de tweede helft van de achttiende eeuw" [Soul and senses: On love and desire between women in the latter half of the eighteenth century]. Ph.D. diss., Rijksuniversiteit Leiden.

Faderman, Lillian. 1981. *Surpassing the Love of Men.* New York: William Morrow.

———. 1991. *Odd Girls and Twilight Lovers: A History of Lesbian Life in Twentieth-Century America.* New York: Columbia University Press.

Feinberg, Leslie. 1996. *Transgender Warriors: Making History from Joan of Arc to RuPaul.* Boston: Beacon Press.

Franzen, Trisha. 1993. "Differences and Identities: Feminism and the Albuquerque Lesbian Community." *Signs:Journal of Women in Culture and Society* 18, no. 4:891–906.

Freedman, Estelle B. 1987. "'Uncontrolled Desires': The Response to the Sexual Psychopath, 1920–1960." *Journal of American History* 74:83–106.

———. 1996. *Maternal Justice: Miriam Van Waters and the Female Reform Tradition.* Chicago: University of Chicago Press.

———. 1998. "'The Burning of Letters Continues': Elusive Identities and the Historical Construction of Sexuality." *Journal of Women's History* 9, no. 4:181–200.

Freeman, Susan. n.d. "From the Lesbian Nation to the Cincinnati Lesbian Community: Moving toward a Politics of Location." *Journal of the History of Sexuality.* Forthcoming.

Friday, Chris. 1994. *Organizing Asian American Labor: The Pacific Coast Canned-Salmon Industry, 1870–1942.* Philadelphia: Temple University Press.

Gamson, Joshua. 1998. *Freaks Talk Back: Tabloid Talk Shows and Sexual Nonconformity.* Chicago: University of Chicago Press.

Garber, Eric. 1989. "A Spectacle in Color: The Lesbian and Gay Subculture of Jazz Age Harlem." In *Hidden from History: Reclaiming the Gay and Lesbian Past,* edited by Martin Bauml Duberman, Martha Vicinus, and George Chauncey Jr., 318–31. New York: New American Library.

Gilbert, Arthur N. 1976. "Buggery and the British Navy, 1700–1861." *Journal of Social History* 10:72–98.

Godbeer, Richard. 1995. " 'The Cry of Sodom': Discourse, Intercourse, and Desire in Colonial New England." *William and Mary Quarterly,* 3d ser., 52:259–84.

Goldman, Marion S. 1981. *Gold Diggers and Silver Miners: Prostitution and Social Life on the Comstock Lode.* Ann Arbor: University of Michigan Press.

Gorn, Elliott J. 1986. *The Manly Art: Bare-Knuckle Prize-Fighting in America.* Ithaca: Cornell University Press.

Greenberg, David F. 1988. *The Construction of Homosexuality.* Chicago: University of Chicago Press.

Gutiérrez, Ramón A. 1991. *When Jesus Came, the Corn Mothers Went Away: Marriage, Sexuality, and Power in New Mexico, 1500–1846.* Berkeley: University of California Press.

Haeberle, Erwin J. 1984. "A Movement of Inverts: An Early Plan for a Homosexual Organization in the United States." *Journal of Homosexuality* 10:127–33.

Halperin, David M. 1989. "Sex before Sexuality: Pederasty, Politics, and Power in Classical Athens." In *Hidden from History: Reclaiming the Gay and Lesbian Past,* edited by Martin Bauml Duberman, Martha Vicinus, and George Chauncey Jr., 37–53. New York: New American Library.

Hansen, Karen V. 1995. " 'No *Kisses* Is Like Youres': An Erotic Friendship between Two African-American Women during the Mid-Nineteenth Century." *Gender and History* 7 (August): 153–82.

Hawkeswood, William G. 1997. *One of the Children: Gay Black Men in Harlem.* Berkeley: University of California Press.

Herdt, Gilbert. 1981. *Guardians of the Flutes.* New York: McGraw-Hill.

Hinsch, Bret. 1990. *Passions of the Cut Sleeve: The Male Homosexual Tradition in China.* Berkeley: University of California Press.

The History Project. 1998. *Improper Bostonians: Lesbian and Gay History from the Puritans to Playland.* Boston: Beacon Press.

Holloway, Pippa. 1997. "Searching for Southern Lesbian History." In *Women of the American South: A Multicultural Reader,* edited by Christie Anne Farnham, 258–72. New York: New York University Press.

Horowitz, Helen Lefkowitz. 1994. *The Power and Passion of M. Carey Thomas.* New York: Alfred A. Knopf.

Howard, John. 1997a. *Carryin' on in the Lesbian and Gay South.* New York: New York University Press.

———. 1997b. "Place and Movement in Gay American History: A

Case from the Post–World War II South." In *Creating a Place for Ourselves: Lesbian, Gay, and Bisexual Community Histories,* edited by Brett Beemyn, 211–25. New York: Routledge.

Hull, Gloria T. 1987. *Color, Sex, and Poetry: Three Women Writers of the Harlem Renaissance.* Bloomington: Indiana University Press.

Huussen, Arend H., Jr. 1989. "Sodomy in the Dutch Republic during the Eighteenth Century." In *Hidden from History: Reclaiming the Gay and Lesbian Past,* edited by Martin Bauml Duberman, Martha Vicinus, and George Chauncey Jr., 141–49. New York: New American Library.

Jacobs, Sue Ellen, Wesley Thomas, and Sabine Lang, eds. 1997. *Two-Spirit People: Native American Gender Identity, Sexuality, and Spirituality.* Urbana: University of Illinois Press.

Johnson, David K. 1993. "Queer Life/Queer Words: The Culture of Gay Male Desire in 1930s Chicago." Unpublished paper in author's possession.

———. 1997. "The Kids of Fairytown: Gay Male Culture on Chicago's Near North Side in the 1930s." In *Creating a Place for Ourselves: Lesbian, Gay, and Bisexual Communities,* edited by Brett Beemyn, 97–111. New York: Routledge.

Katz, Jonathan Ned. 1976. *Gay American History.* New York: Thomas Y. Crowell.

———. 1983. *Gay/Lesbian Almanac: A New Documentary.* New York: Harper and Row.

———. 1995. *The Invention of Heterosexuality.* New York: Dutton.

Kennedy, Elizabeth Lapovsky. 1996. " 'But We Would Never Talk about It': The Structures of Lesbian Discretion in South Dakota, 1928–1933." In *Inventing Lesbian Cultures in America,* edited by Ellen Lewin, 15–39. Boston: Beacon Press.

Kennedy, Elizabeth Lapovsky, and Madeline D. Davis. 1993. *Boots of Leather, Slippers of Gold: The History of a Lesbian Community.* New York: Routledge.

Kinsey, Alfred C., Wardell B. Pomeroy, and Clyde E. Martin. 1948. *Sexual Behavior in the Human Male.* Philadelphia: W. B Saunders.

Kinsey, Alfred C., Wardell B. Pomeroy, Clyde E. Martin, and Paul H. Gebhard. 1953. *Sexual Behavior in the Human Female.* Philadelphia: W. B. Saunders.

Kissack, Terrance. 1995. "Freaking Fag Revolutionaries: New York's Gay Liberation Front, 1969–1971." *Radical History Review* 62 (spring): 104–34.

Knowlton, Elizabeth W. 1997. " 'Only a Woman Like Yourself'—Rebecca Alice Baldy, Dutiful Daughter, Stalwart Sister, and Lesbian

Lover of Nineteenth-Century Georgia." In *Carryin' on in the Lesbian and Gay South,* edited by John Howard, 34–53. New York: New York University Press.

Koedt, Anne, Ellen Levine, and Anita Rapone, eds. 1973. *Radical Feminism.* New York: Quadrangle.

Levine, Martin P. 1998. *Gay Macho: The Life and Death of the Homosexual Clone.* Edited and with an introduction by Michael S. Kimmel. New York: New York University Press.

Lister, Anne. 1988. *I Know My Own Heart: The Diaries of Anne Lister (1791–1840).* Edited by Helena Whitbread. London: Virago.

———. 1992. *No Priest but Love: The Journals of Anne Lister from 1824–1826.* Edited by Helena Whitbread. New York: New York University Press.

Lunbeck, Elizabeth. 1994. *The Psychiatric Persuasion: Knowledge, Gender, and Power in Modern America.* Princeton: Princeton University Press.

Mason, Jack, and Donald Guimary. 1981. "Asian Labor Contractors in the Alaskan Canned Salmon Industry, 1880–1937." *Labor History* 23, no. 3:377–97.

Meyer, Leisa D. 1996. *Creating GI Jane: Sexuality and Power in the Women's Army Corps during World War II.* New York: Columbia University Press.

Meyerowitz, Joanne. 1988. *Women Adrift: Independent Wage Earners in Chicago, 1880–1930.* Chicago: University of Chicago Press.

Middlebrook, Diane Wood. 1998. *Suits Me: The Double Life of Billy Tipton.* New York: Houghton Mifflin.

Miller, Heather Lee. 1997. "A Historical Sisterhood under the Sexologists' Gaze: Prostitutes and Lesbians, 1840–1940." Unpublished paper in author's possession.

Moon, Michael. 1987. " 'The Gentle Boy from the Dangerous Classes': Pederasty, Domesticity, and Capitalism in Horatio Alger." *Representations* 19:87–110.

Moraga, Cherríe. 1983. *Loving in the War Years: Lo Que Nunca Pasó sus Labios.* Boston: South End Press.

Moraga, Cherríe, and Amber Hollibaugh. 1983. "What We're Rolling around in Bed With: Sexual Silences in Feminism." In *Powers of Desire: The Politics of Sexuality,* edited by Ann Snitow, Christine Stansell, and Sharon Thompson, 394–405. New York: Monthly Review Press.

Moum, Barbara A. 1992. "The Stonewall Rebellion: An Investigation of Mainstream Press Coverage." Unpublished paper in author's possession.

Mumford, Kevin J. 1996. "Homosex Changes: Race, Cultural Geography, and the Emergence of the Gay." *American Quarterly* 48, no. 3:395–414.

Nestle, Joan. 1981. "Butch–Fem Relationships: Sexual Courage in the 1950s." *Heresies* 3, no. 4:21–24.

———. 1984. "The Fem Question." In *Pleasure and Danger: Exploring Female Sexuality,* edited by Carole S. Vance, 232–41. Boston: Routledge and Kegan Paul.

———. 1987. "Lesbians and Prostitutes: A Historical Sisterhood." In *Sex Work: Writings by Women in the Sex Industry,* edited by Frédérique Delacoste and Priscilla Alexander, 231–47. San Francisco: Cleis Press.

———. 1992. *The Persistent Desire: A Femme-Butch Reader.* Boston: Alyson.

———. 1993. "Excerpts from the Oral History of Mabel Hampton." *Signs: Journal of Women in Culture and Society* 18, no. 4:925–35.

Newton, Esther. 1993. *Cherry Grove, Fire Island: Sixty Years in America's First Gay and Lesbian Town.* Boston: Beacon Press.

Ng, Vivien W. 1989. "Homosexuality and the State in Late Imperial China." In *Hidden from History: Reclaiming the Gay and Lesbian Past,* edited by Martin Bauml Duberman, Martha Vicinus, and George Chauncey Jr., 76–89. New York: New American Library.

Norton, Mary Beth. 1997. "Communal Definitions of Gendered Identity in Seventeenth-Century English America." In *Through a Glass Darkly: Reflections on Personal Identity in Early America,* edited by Ronald Hoffman, Mechal Sobel, and Fredrika J. Teute, 40–66. Chapel Hill: University of North Carolina Press.

Norton, Rictor. 1992. *Mother Clap's Molly House: The Gay Subculture in England, 1700–1830.* London: Gay Men's Press.

Orleck, Annelise. 1995. *Common Sense and a Little Fire: Women and Working-Class Politics in the United States, 1900–1965.* Chapel Hill: University of North Carolina Press.

Padgug, Robert. 1989. "Sexual Matters: Rethinking Sexuality in History." In *Hidden from History: Reclaiming the Gay and Lesbian Past,* edited by Martin Bauml Duberman, Martha Vicinus, and George Chauncey Jr., 54–64. New York: New American Library.

Perry, Adele. 1997. " 'Fair Ones of a Purer Caste': White Women and Colonialism in Nineteenth-Century British Columbia." *Feminist Studies* 23 (fall): 501–24.

Quinn, D. Michael. 1996. *Same-Sex Dynamics among Nineteenth-Century Americans: A Mormon Example.* Urbana: University of Illinois Press.

Retzloff, Tim. 1997. "Cars and Bars: Assembling Gay Men in Postwar Flint, Michigan." In *Creating a Place for Ourselves: Lesbian, Gay, and Bisexual Community Histories,* edited by Brett Beemyn, 226–52. New York: Routledge.

Rey, Michael. 1985. "Parisian Homosexuals Create a Lifestyle, 1700–1750: The Police Archives." *Eighteenth-Century Life,* n.s., 9, no. 3:179–91.

Reynolds, David S. 1995. *Walt Whitman's America: A Cultural Biography.* New York: Alfred A. Knopf.

Roscoe, Will. 1988. "The Zuni Man-Woman." *Out/look* 1 (summer): 56–67.

Rothblum, Esther D., and Kathleen A. Brehony, eds. 1993. *Boston Marriages: Romantic but Asexual Relationships among Contemporary Lesbians.* Amherst: University of Massachusetts Press.

Rotundo, E. Anthony. 1989. "Romantic Friendship: Male Intimacy and Middle-Class Youth in the Northern United States, 1800–1900." *Journal of Social History* 23:1–25.

Rupp, Leila J. 1997. "Sexuality and Politics in the Early Twentieth Century: The Case of the International Women's Movement." *Feminist Studies* 23, no. 3:577–605.

Russell, Ida, ed. 1993. *Jeb and Dash: A Diary of Gay Life, 1918–1945.* Boston: Faber and Faber.

Russo, Vito. 1987. *The Celluloid Closet: Homosexuality in the Movies.* Rev. ed. New York: Harper and Row.

Sahli, Nancy. 1979. "Smashing: Women's Relationships before the Fall." *Chrysalis* 8:17–27.

Sams, Conway Whittle. 1916. *The Conquest of Virginia, the Forest Primeval: An Account Based on Original Documents of the Indians of That Portion of the Continent in Which Was Established the First English Colony in America.* New York: G. P. Putnam's Sons.

San Francisco Lesbian and Gay History Project. 1989. " 'She Even Chewed Tobacco': A Pictorial Narrative of Passing Women in American." In *Hidden from History: Reclaiming the Gay and Lesbian Past,* edited by Martin Bauml Duberman, Martha Vicinus, and George Chauncey Jr., 183–94. New York: New American Library.

Saslow, James M. 1989. "Homosexuality in the Renaissance: Behavior, Identity, and Artistic Expression." In *Hidden from History: Reclaiming the Gay and Lesbian Past,* edited by Martin Bauml Duberman, Martha Vicinus, and George Chauncey Jr., 90–105. New York: New American Library.

Shively, Charles. 1987. *Calamus Lovers: Walt Whitman's Working-Class Camerados.* San Francisco: Gay Sunshine Press.

Silvera, Makeda. 1992. "Man Royals and Sodomites: Some Thoughts on the Invisibility of Afro-Caribbean Lesbians." *Feminist Studies* 18, no. 3:521–32.

Smith-Rosenberg, Carroll. 1975. "The Female World of Love and Ritual: Relations between Women in Nineteenth-Century America." *Signs: Journal of Women in Culture and Society* 1, no.1:1–29.

———. 1985. *Disorderly Conduct: Visions of Gender in Victorian America.* New York: Oxford University Press.

———. 1989. "Discourses of Sexuality and Subjectivity: The New Woman, 1870–1936." In *Hidden from History: Reclaiming the Gay and Lesbian Past,* edited by Martin Bauml Duberman, Martha Vicinus, and George Chauncey Jr., 264–80. New York: New American Library.

Stein, Edward. 1990. *Forms of Desire: Sexual Orientation and the Social Constructionist Controversy.* New York: Routledge.

Stein, Marc. 1994. "The City of Sisterly and Brotherly Loves: The Making of Lesbian and Gay Movements in Greater Philadelphia, 1948–72." Ph.D diss., University of Pennsylvania.

———. n.d. *City of Sisterly and Brotherly Loves: Making Lesbian and Gay History in Philadelphia, 1945–72.* Chicago: University of Chicago Press. In press.

Taylor, Verta. 1980. Book review. *Journal of Marriage and the Family* 42 (February): 224–28.

Taylor, Verta, and Leila J. Rupp. 1993. "Women's Culture and Lesbian Feminist Activism: A Reconsideration of Cultural Feminism." *Signs: Journal of Women in Culture and Society* 19, no. 3:32–61.

Terry, Jennifer. 1991. "Theorizing Deviant Historiography." *Differences: A Journal of Feminist Cultural Studies* 3, no. 2:55–74.

Thorpe, Roey. 1997. "The Changing Face of Lesbian Bars in Detroit, 1938–1965." In *Creating a Place for Ourselves,* edited by Brett Beemyn, 165–81. New York: Routledge.

Trexler, Richard. 1995. *Sex and Conquest: Gendered Violence, Political Order, and the European Conquest of the Americas.* Ithaca: Cornell University Press.

Trumbach, Randolph. 1989. "The Birth of the Queen: Sodomy and the Emergence of Gender Equality in Modern Culture, 1660–1750." In *Hidden from History: Reclaiming the Gay and Lesbian Past,* edited by Martin Bauml Duberman, Martha Vicinus, and George Chauncey Jr., 129–40. New York: New American Library.

Truscott, Lucian, IV. 1969. "Gay Power Comes to Sheridan Square." *Village Voice,* July 3, 1, 18.

Ullman, Sharon R. 1995. " 'The Twentieth Century Way': Female Im-

personation and Sexual Practice in Turn-of-the-Century America."
Journal of the History of Sexuality 5, no. 4:573–600.

Vance, Carole S. 1989. "Social Construction Theory: Problems in the
History of Sexuality." In *Homosexuality, Which Homosexuality? In-
ternational Conference on Gay and Lesbian Studies,* edited by Dennis
Altman et al., 13–34. Amsterdam: Dekker/Schorer.

Wat, Eric C. 1996. "Preserving the Paradox: Stories from a *Gay-Loh.*
In *Asian American Sexualities: Dimensions of the Gay and Lesbian
Experience,* edited by Russell Leong, 71–80. New York: Routledge.

Weiss, Andrea, and Greta Schiller. 1988. *Before Stonewall: The Making
of a Gay and Lesbian Community.* Tallahassee, Fla.: Naiad Press.

Weiss, John McNish. 1996. "The Corps of Colonial Marines 1814–16:
A Summary." *Immigrants and Minorities* 5, no. 2:80–90.

Westermeier, Clifford. 1974. "Cowboy Sexuality: A Historical No-No?"
Red River Valley Historical Review 2:92–113.

White, Kevin. 1993. *The First Sexual Revolution: The Emergence of Male
Heterosexuality in Modern America.* New York: New York University
Press.

Williams, Walter L. 1986. *The Spirit and the Flesh: Sexual Diversity in
American Indian Culture.* Boston: Beacon Press.

Wright, Les, ed. 1997. *The Bear Book: Readings in the History and
Evolution of a Gay Male Subculture.* New York: Harrington Park
Press.

Wu, Judy Tzu-Chun. 1997. "Beyond Marriage and Motherhood: The
Sexual Life of Dr. Margaret Chung." Unpublished paper in author's
possession.

Index

Page numbers of photographs are in italic.